MW00697253

Mediterranean Cookbook Bundle

3 Books in 1

150 Mediterranean Diet Meal and Salad Recipes

By

Patrick Smith

ISBN-10: 1503291537
ISBN-13: 978-1503291539

Contents

Fruit Salads 145

Pasta Salads 155

Section 1: The Diet

The Mediterranean diet is highly popular among health buffs and those trying to lose weight. It is composed of the traditional foods and beverages of the countries surrounding the Mediterranean Sea, including healthy eating and cooking habits such as the following:

- *Making use of good fats* such as extra virgin olive oil, avocados, olives, and sunflower seeds.

- *Reserving the consumption of sweets* during special occasions only.

- *Watching meat size portions.* There are many ways to add a lot of flavor to a dish without the need for an oversized portion of meat. For example, garnish a pasta dish with chopped prosciutto or include tiny strips of sirloin to sautéed vegetables. For main courses, an adequate portion is a maximum of 3.5 ounces (100 grams) of chicken or lean meat.

- *Preparing and eating meals with no meat content* at least once a week.

- *Consuming nutrient-rich eggs and dairy products* throughout the week.

- *Consuming seafood two times a week.* Fish and shellfish such as shrimp, sardines, salmon, herring, and tuna are high in omega-3 fatty acids, which are very beneficial to the health of the brain and heart.

- *Eating breakfast daily.* It is true that breakfast is the most important meal, because what you eat at breakfast will provide most of the energy you need for the whole day. This is why you should include foods that are rich in fiber in your breakfast, such as whole grains and fruits, together with good proteins such as those from dairy products and eggs. A good breakfast will also help in making you feel full for longer amount of time.

- *Eating lots of vegetables.* Vegetables are the foundation of all meals in the Mediterranean diet.

A substantial amount of scientific research carried out throughout the last six decades show that the Mediterranean diet is one of the world's healthiest ways of eating. Whenever researchers study any single food of the Mediterranean diet, such as extra virgin olive oil, a specific fish, or nut, they discover that its health benefits are linked to the Mediterranean diet as a whole, and cannot be connected to just one specific ingredient.

In other words, there is not a single secret ingredient to good health. Eating an array of whole foods and foods that underwent minimal processing coupled with regular physical activity are the essential concepts of the Mediterranean diet.

The food pyramid shown below illustrates the traditional foods and beverages that, together, make up the balanced and healthy Mediterranean diet. Many of the foods included in this pyramid can also be found in other dietary pyramids. The main difference is in how frequently some of the foods are consumed. Almost any food can be included in a healthy and balanced diet, but the portion size of each food you eat and how often you eat various foods dramatically affect your overall health.

The top of the pyramid includes sweets and red meat. These make up the foods that you should only eat in small amounts. Red meats should not be eaten often and it is better to go for small portions of lean cuts, like flank, T-bone, strip, tenderloin, shoulder, and round. As mentioned earlier, as a main course, the ideal portion size should be 3.5 ounces (100 grams) or less. As for sweets, eat them only as a treat or during special occasions.

The next layer of the pyramid includes eggs, poultry, cheese, and yogurt (dairy products). These make up a focal part of the Mediterranean diet and you should eat them in moderate portion sizes plenty of times per week. For example, you should consume cheese regularly but in small amounts only.

The third layer of the pyramid includes fish and other kinds of seafood. These have their own section because they are chief protein sources. Shellfish like clams, shrimp, oysters, and mussels are high in omega-3 fatty acids, which are extremely beneficial to the heart and brain.

Fish such as sardines, salmon, herring, and tuna have the same benefits. Seafood should be consumed at least two times per week.

The next two layers of the pyramid include herbs, beans, vegetables, fruits, and whole grains. These make up the heart of the Mediterranean diet. Every meal should be based on legumes, spices, herbs, whole grains, vegetables and fruits. Meanwhile, the primary source of dietary fat is extra virgin olive oil, and should be used for almost all baking and cooking, and for dressing vegetables and salads.

All of this needs to go along with exercise. Good exercise is extremely vital for your overall health. This includes laborious workout such as aerobics, running, and jogging, less strenuous activities such as meditation and yoga, and simple physical activity such as walking, household chores, walking back and forth while talking on the phone, and taking the stairs instead of the escalator or elevator.

Also, the Mediterranean diet includes water as its main beverage. Eight to ten glasses of water should be consumed every day. This it is vital for the body to be properly hydrated, it boosts your energy, and it contributes to your overall health and well-being.

In contrast to many diets out there, the Mediterranean diet is not about constricting the amount of food you eat. Instead, it allows you to eat a lot and feel full by preparing and consuming healthy and delectable means with your family and friends as part of your regular way of living. The secret is to prepare meals with whole foods that underwent minimal processing, coupled with regular exercise. The ingredients needed are extremely rich in flavor, offer a lot of health benefits, and are very easy to find.

Health Benefits of the Mediterranean Diet

The Mediterranean diet lifestyle is one of the healthiest diets in the world. In fact, it is one of the most researched and extensively acclaimed diets as proven by a substantial amount of scientific studies conducted over the past sixty years. The following are just some of the amazing health benefits offered by this way of eating:

Numerous studies have shown that following the Mediterranean diet has the following benefits.

1. Improved mental and physical health

2. Improved symptoms of sleep apnea

3. Lower risk for some types of cancer

4. Improvement in bone and teeth health

5. Prevention of Parkinson's disease

6. Slower decline of brain health due to aging, thus lowering the risk of Alzheimer's disease

7. Lower chances of developing depression and similar illnesses in older age

8. Inflammation is reduced and the flowing levels of anti-oxidants are increased

9. Lower risk of developing type 2 diabetes

10. Better management of blood sugar levels in people diagnosed with type 2 diabetes

11. Lower risk of having a heart attack or stroke

12. Lower risk of developing heart diseases

13. The Mediterranean diet in itself tends to induce weight loss, because the portion sizes of certain food types are limited, and the meals are generally savored and enjoyed, not consumed hastily.

The following are some of the numerous highly nutritional foods making up this diet:

Whole grains

These are rich in protein, fiber, and other nutrients. The carbohydrates they contain are the "good" carbohydrates and are a significant choice for a healthy diet. The popular whole grains for the Mediterranean diet include farro, whole wheat couscous, bulgur, brown rice, quinoa, and barley.

Wine

Wine is rich in strong antioxidants coming from grape seeds and skins and has been proven to lower the risk of majority of diseases associated with aging. Low amounts of alcohol improve brain function, while excessive amounts harm the brain and cause fatty liver disease. Men can consume up to two glasses of wine per day, whereas woman should not go beyond one glass per day. For non-wine drinkers, a substitute is 100% organic grape juice.

Seeds and Nuts

Not only do nuts such as walnuts, almonds, hazelnuts, peanuts, pecans, pistachios, and pine nuts, make a good and easy snack, but they are also rich in fiber, protein, and healthy fats that are good for the heart. Seeds are also extremely healthy and go well with roasted vegetables and salads. Good examples include fennel seeds, chia seeds, flax seeds, sunflower seeds and sesame seeds.

Beans

Beans such as white beans, kidney beans, and chickpeas are rich in fiber and protein. They are an excellent substitute for meat and great for vegetarian meals. If you are using canned beans, make sure to drain the liquids and rinse the beans well to wash away the excess sodium.

Yogurt

Yogurt is very high in protein and calcium, which is good for protecting and strengthening bones. It also contains good bacteria that promote healthy digestion. It is recommended to go for Greek yogurt, because it contains twice the amount of protein of regular yogurt, and it also has a nice, tangy flavor.

Tomatoes

These are rich in lycopene and vitamin C. Lycopene is a powerful antioxidant that helps in combating chronic illnesses and promote a healthy immune system.

Fish and seafood

In the Mediterranean diet, fish and seafood should be consumed twice per week. Fish contains a lot of healthy fats. Fish such as mackerel, sardines, tuna, and salmon are high in omega-3 fatty acids, which are beneficial to the health of the heart and brain.

Avocados

These are rich in vitamin E, healthy monounsaturated fats, and fiber. In addition, they are available any time of the year. You can incorporate avocados in salads, use them in dips, or just eat them on their own!

Frequently Asked Questions

The Mediterranean diet uses mainly olive oil and also includes nuts. Aren't these high in fats?

When talking about fats in food, you should know two very important things. First, determine the kind of fat. Second, determine the amount of fat. For example, even healthy fats, if taken in high amounts, can result in weight gain.

Saturated fats are typically found in foods that came from animal sources, such as eggs, dairy products, and meat. Trans fats are artificial and can be found in processed foods. They clog arteries and are a major cause for heart disease. After decades of making people sick, trans fats were finally banned by the American Food and Drug Administration at end of 2013. However, keep in mind that it will take time for this to be implemented for all processed foods out there.

The ideal thing to do is stay away or restrict your intake of trans fats or saturated fats, because these kinds of fats can increase LDL-C (low-density lipoprotein cholesterol) aka "bad" cholesterol, and lower the HDL-C (high-density lipoprotein cholesterol) aka "good" cholesterol.

On the other hand, the fats contained in nuts and olive oil are polyunsaturated fats and monounsaturated fats, which are *healthy* fats that do not increase LDL-C. Then again, do not forget that olive oil and nuts are high in calories too, so you should consume them in reasonable quantities.

An even better example for healthy saturated fats are coconut products. Though not part of the Mediterranean diet, coconut is extremely healthy, and it is advisable to replace butter/margarine with coconut oil.

What are some tips for beginners of the Mediterranean diet?

It is best to make a meal plan for all your meals and snacks for every week in advance. This way, you will know which foods to stock up in your kitchen, and you will be motivated to follow the meals you planned.

Also, always substitute olive oil or coconut oil for meals that call for butter. Never use margarine.

If possible, consider consulting a professional dietitian so you can be guided more accurately in the food choices suitable for your lifestyle and culture.

Why is it called the Mediterranean diet?

This way of eating is characteristic of the countries which surround the Mediterranean Sea, such as Lebanon, Libya, Croatia, Israel, Greece, Albania, Algeria, Turkey, Tunisia, Malta, Syria, Morocco, Egypt, Italy, France, and Spain.

Will I always feel hungry once I start following the Mediterranean diet?

No. The Mediterranean diet is not a diet wherein you will starve yourself. Rather, it is a lifestyle. It involves eating whole grains, nuts, beans, fish, vegetables fruits, and meat in proper proportions and frequency, coupled with regular physical activity. As long as you follow the diet properly, you can still get to eat a lot and feel full longer while staying healthy and maintaining or losing your weight.

Is it easy to follow the Mediterranean Diet correctly?

Yes, because you do not count calories, but simply eat good foods. The food choices are diverse and have a great taste. Here are some tips for this diet:

Consume small portions of cheese and yogurt every day. For example, feta cheese makes a great ingredient for salads, which means that even a salad can be a vessel for your daily cheese intake.

Go for lean meat such as chicken, turkey, fish, and beans as your source of protein. You can enjoy red meat during special occasions.

Consume sweets during special occasions or as a treat.

Base your every meal on whole grains, vegetables, fruits, nuts, beans, spices, and herbs.

Go for healthy fats such as those found in fish like tuna, salmon, sardines, and mackerel, avocados, nuts, extra virgin olive oil, and extra virgin coconut oil.

Why should I abide by the Mediterranean diet?

Studies conducted over the last six decades have shown that the Mediterranean diet is one of the healthiest diets in the world. In addition, it offers diverse food choices that are rich in flavor.

Is the Mediterranean diet is just another fad diet?

No, the Mediterranean diet is a lifestyle. It is a way of eating that is sustainable and has been shown to improve health and lower the risk of chronic illnesses.

Is the Mediterranean diet is a new way of eating?

No, the Mediterranean diet started in the 1940s. Back then, a researcher named Ancel Keys discovered that most of the people in Mediterranean countries had very low rates of heart disease and were living longer lives than people in the northern part of Europe.

Does the Mediterranean diet involve foods that are foreign and hard to access?

No. Almost every food included in the Mediterranean diet pyramid can be found in your local grocery store. In fact, all you need are vegetables, fruits, whole grains, dairy products, fish, nuts, and olive oil. The next chapter will show you which foods you should stock up in your kitchen so you can easily prepare a Mediterranean meal at any time.

May I consume sweets or meats if I follow this diet?

Red meats and sweets can be consumed during special occasions or just occasionally. Lean meat such as chicken, turkey, and fish are recommended to be eaten more often.

Is it true that I will lose weight if I follow this diet?

The Mediterranean diet is not a way of eating intended to make you lose weight, but weight loss is one of its added benefits if it is followed properly. This is because the diet involves eating healthy meals in proper portions coupled with regular physical activity.

You are most likely to reach and maintain your own normal weight, not going above or below that. There is a certain weight that your brain considers normal for your body, something that is different for every one of us. If you eat too much and do not have an eating disorder, your brain will try to regulate your metabolism and hunger to bring your weight back down. If you eat too little, like in most diets, your brain will believe there is a famine and you are starving. It will do all it can to get you back to normal levels: this is why most diets do not work and people end up with more weight than before.

Being healthy is not about being slim, it is about keeping what your brain considers to be the normal weight for your body.

With the Mediterranean diet, you give your body exactly what it really wants: healthy foods in enough quantity.

What Should Be in Your Kitchen

In your pantry

Vinegars: white wine vinegar, red wine vinegar, fig vinegar, apple cider vinegar, champagne vinegar, balsamic vinegar, vinaigrette

Canned tomatoes: sun-dried tomatoes, diced tomatoes, tomato sauce, tomato paste

Seeds: sunflower seeds, sesame seeds, flax seeds, fennel seeds

Salt: table salt, sea salt, kosher salt

Red wine

Potatoes (all kinds)

Pastas (all kinds, including whole grain pasta)

Olives (black olives, Kalamata olives)

Nuts: walnuts, pistachios, pine nuts, peanuts, hazelnuts, pecans, almonds

Raw honey

Herbs and spices: Italian seasoning, dried oregano, dried basil, turmeric powder, cumin seeds, ground cinnamon, garlic powder, onion powder, curry powder, dill, rosemary, thyme, parsley, black pepper, bay leaves, fresh garlic, fresh onions, coriander, sage, saffron, parsley, mint, ground black pepper, crushed red peppers, chili flakes, cayenne pepper, paprika, ginger

Grains: quinoa, rice, polenta, oats, millet, farro, couscous

Dried fruits: prunes, raisins, figs dates, cranberries, cherries, blueberries, raspberries, apricots

Crackers: whole-wheat/whole-grain crackers that contain two to three grams of fiber per serving

Oatmeal and cereals

Capers: They will last for up to six months in the refrigerator.

Canned seafood: tuna, sardines, salmon, clams, anchovies

Breads: pita, focaccia, bread crumbs, and other whole grain or whole wheat breads.

Beans: lentils, kidney beans, white beans, fava, cannellini, and chickpeas.

On your counter

Extra virgin olive oil. You can also use coconut oil, due to its immense health benefits.

Fresh tomatoes: plum tomatoes, cherry tomatoes, grape tomatoes, Roma tomatoes

Fresh fruits: tangerines, pomegranates, pears, peaches, apples, plums, bananas, dates, nectarines, melons, oranges, limes, lemons, grapefruit, figs, clementines, cherries, apricots, and avocados. These fruits are best stored at room temperature.

In your freezer

Gelato

Sorbet

Frozen chicken stock

Frozen vegetables

Frozen seafood

Frozen meat and poultry

Frozen fruits

Yogurt

Sparkling wine and white wine

Vegetables

Tapenade

Pickles

Pesto

Mustard

Fruits: grapes, berries, mangoes

Eggs

Cheese (hard and soft varieties): feta cheese, Parmesan, mozzarella, goat cheese

Section 2: Meal Recipes

Breakfast Recipes

1. Vegetarian Omelet

In the Mediterranean countries, eggs are eaten often and make a good choice for breakfast, because they offer a lot of vitamins, minerals, and protein. Though eggs contain high levels of cholesterol, consuming eggs in moderation does not have any established harmful effects on cardiovascular health. This recipe is for a simple Mediterranean vegetarian omelet that is easy to make, yet healthy and delicious!

2 tbs fresh **parsley leaves** (chopped)
½ cup **goat cheese** (crumbled)
6 **eggs**
¼ cup **artichoke hearts**
¼ green **olives** (pitted, chopped)
1 **Roma tomato** (diced)
2 cups fresh bulbs of **fennel** (sliced thinly)
1 tbs extra virgin **olive oil**
¼ tsp **table salt**
½ tsp **black pepper** (ground)

Makes: 4 servings
Calories: 132 per serving

Marinate the artichoke hearts in water for a few minutes, then rinse and drain thoroughly. Chop them into small pieces and set aside.

Wash the fresh parsley leaves and rinse thoroughly. Set aside 2 tbs of the chopped parsley leaves. Slice the fennel bulbs into thin slices, then set aside.

Preheat the oven to 325 F (160 °C).

In a large skillet, heat the extra virgin olive oil. Once hot, sauté the sliced fennel for about 5 minutes, or until tender.

Add in the chopped artichoke hearts, pitted olives, and diced tomato and sauté for an additional 3 minutes, or until soft.

In a large bowl, whisk the eggs. Add the table salt and freshly ground black pepper and whisk again until the seasonings are well distributed.

Pour the egg mixture into the skillet containing the sautéed vegetables and stir using a wooden spoon for 2 minutes. Transfer the omelet to a baking tray.

Crumble the goat cheese over the omelet and bake in the oven for about 5 minutes, or until the eggs are cooked through and the cheese has melted.

Garnish with chopped parsley leaves on top. Serve immediately.

Enjoy!

2. Breakfast Egg Wraps

This is a simple dish of scrambled eggs with feta cheese covered in tortilla wraps. It has a light, salty and tangy flavor thanks to the feta cheese, which complements the eggs perfectly.

Tortilla wraps
2 tbs **spring onions** (minced)
2 tbs **red peppers** (roasted)
¾ cup **feta cheese** (crumbled)
½ tsp **dried oregano**
½ tsp **dried basil**
¼ tsp **garlic powder**
¼ tsp **salt** and **black pepper** (ground)
¼ cup **light sour cream**
6 **eggs**
1 tsp extra virgin **olive oil**

Makes: 4 servings
Calories: 245 per serving

Chop the red peppers into small pieces, then sauté in a skillet for a few minutes. Set aside.

Whisk the eggs on a small mixing bowl. Add in the garlic powder, dried oregano, dried basil, black pepper, table salt, and sour cream. Whisk together until well combined. Add the feta cheese.

Heat the extra virgin olive oil in a skillet. Once hot, pour in the egg mixture and cook until most of the eggs are cooked but overall still slightly wet. Add in the chopped spring onions and the red peppers. Stir well until everything has been cooked completely.

If you want, you can garnish the top with additional feta cheese.

Wrap the scrambled eggs in tortilla wraps and serve immediately.

3. Cheese and Zucchini Frittata

In the Mediterranean countries, people usually use frittatas and scrambled eggs to use up leftovers, which is a good idea so nothing will go to waste. Aside from saving you money, it is also an excellent way to add some extra vegetables to your meal.

2 oz. (60 g) **goat cheese** or **feta cheese** (crumbled)
1 **garlic clove** (crushed, minced)
1 tbs extra virgin **olive oil**
1/8 tsp **black pepper** (ground)
¼ tsp **table salt**
2 tbs **skim milk**
8 **eggs**
2 medium-sized **zucchinis**

Makes: 4 servings
Calories: 127 per serving

In a large mixing bowl, whisk the eggs. Add in the ground black pepper, table salt, and skim milk. Whisk again until thoroughly combined. Set aside.

In a large skillet, put in the extra virgin olive oil and heat over medium heat. Once the oil is hot, add in the minced garlic and cook for about half a minute while constantly stirring to prevent it from burning. Then, add the slices of zucchini and continue cooking for about five more minutes.

While the zucchini is being cooked, preheat the oven to 350F (180°C).

Pour the egg mixture onto the zucchini and garlic mixture and stir well for about one minute or until the eggs have reached your desired level of doneness. Transfer the mixture to a circular baking pan. Crumble the goat cheese or feta cheese on top.

Bake in the preheated oven for about 10 to 12 minutes, or until the eggs are fully cooked.

Once done, immediately remove the baking pan from the oven and let it sit for 3 minutes.

Remove the frittata from the baking pan and transfer to a chopping board or a clean wooden surface. Slice the frittata into four equal portions.
You can serve the frittatas immediately or allow it to cool to room temperature before serving.

Enjoy!

4. Breakfast Smoothie

Nothing beats a delicious and refreshing smoothie, especially in summer. Not only is it delicious, but also extremely healthy! This recipe is for a traditional Mediterranean breakfast smoothie, but it is good for any time of the day.

4 **ice cubes**
½ cup **skim milk**
½ cup **beet juice**
1 small **ripe mango** (diced)
1 frozen **banana** (sliced)
½-inch (1.3 cm) fresh **ginger root** (sliced)
2 cups **organic baby spinach**

Makes: 2 servings
Calories: 162 per serving

Cut the ripe mango into three parts and remove the middle part (containing the seed). Peel off the skin and cut the mango into cubes. Set aside.

Prepare the beet juice. If you prefer, you can purchase canned beets at the grocery store that already includes beet juice. However, it is best to make your own beet juice by adding the beets to a juicer.

Once you have the beet juice ready, transfer it to a blender together with other ingredients. Blend until smooth. Consume immediately.

Enjoy!

5. Quinoa Meal

This recipe is for quinoa with a cinnamon and nutty flavor, made even healthier and more delicious by the addition of honey, toasted almonds, apricots, and dates.

5 dried **apricots** (chopped)
2 pitted **dates** (chopped)
2 tbs raw **honey**
1 tsp **vanilla extract**
1 tsp **sea salt**
2 cups **skim milk**
1 cup **quinoa**
1 tsp **cinnamon** (ground)
¼ cup raw **almonds** (chopped)

Makes: 4 servings
Calories: 310 per serving

Heat a skillet over medium heat. Once hot, put in the raw almonds and roast them for 3 to 5 minutes, or until they are golden in color. Set aside.

Heat a large saucepan over medium heat. Put in the quinoa and the ground cinnamon and mix well. Allow them to be heated through. Once done, add in the sea salt and skim milk, then mix well. Increase the heat and let the mixture boil.

Once boiling, reduce to a simmer. Put the lid on and simmer for about fifteen minutes.

Add in the apricots, dates, raw honey, vanilla extract, and half of the roasted almonds. Mix well. Serve immediately in 4 individual bowls.

Top each serving with the remaining toasted almonds.

Enjoy!

6. Potatoes with Bacon and Scrambled Eggs

¼ cup **feta cheese** (crumbled)
3 cups **potatoes** (roasted, quartered)
2 cups fresh **baby spinach leaves**
¼ cup **Kalamata olives**, pitted and chopped
8 strips **bacon** (cooked, crumbled)
1 tbs **extra virgin olive oil**
8 **eggs**
2 tbs **milk**
½ tsp **kosher salt** + ¼ tsp **black pepper**
3 tbs **red peppers** (chopped, roasted)
Seasoning (vegetable broth, garlic salt, pepper, and paprika)

Makes: 4 servings
Calories: 145 per serving

Preheat the oven to 375 F (190°C).

Place the quartered potatoes in bowl. Add enough vegetable broth to thoroughly wet the potatoes. Season with garlic salt, ground pepper and paprika to taste.

Place the potato quarters on a baking sheet and bake for 25 - 30 minutes, or until tender.
Heat olive oil in a skillet over medium heat, then add spinach leaves and cook until wilted. Remove and set aside.

Combine salt, pepper, milk and eggs in a bowl. Stir to combine, then add the mixture to another skillet over medium heat. Scramble the eggs using a spoon or spatula, then add the feta cheese, spinach, olives, bacon, and red peppers. Stir to combine.

Place potatoes in a serving bowl and top with the scrambled eggs and bacon.

Serve immediately and enjoy!

7. Mediterranean Yoghurt

Yoghurt recipes are not only delicious and a treat, they are healthy and make for a nutritious breakfast. You can use any kind of fresh berries for this recipe that you want. My recommendation is blueberries, blackberries, or strawberries.

¼ cup organic **honey**
4 cups plain **Greek yogurt**
2 cups fresh **berries** of your choice
1 cup uncooked **grano**
¼ cup organic **honey**
¼ tsp **kosher salt**

Makes: 8 servings
Calories: 225 per serving

Prepare the grano on the evening before serving by soaking it in 6 cups of water overnight.

In the morning, drain the grano, place it in a saucepan, add 6 cups of water and set heat to high. Once boiling, reduce heat and simmer for 25 minutes, or until the grano is tender.

Remove from heat and drain. Stir in honey and salt, then allow it to cool.

Place ¼ cup of the Greek yoghurt in a serving glass, preferably a parfait glass. Add 3 tbs of grano and 2 tbs of your chosen berries to the yoghurt. Continue making layers until the glass is full, then repeat with another glass.

There should be enough material to prepare 8 glasses. Alternatively, you can make 1 glass bowl of yoghurt and layers.

Enjoy!

8. Sweet Breakfast Muesli

This Mediterranean muesli is quick and very easy to make. It is
delicious and healthy. If you prefer it less sweet, take less honey.

3 tbs **pitted dates** (chopped)
3 tbs dried **apricots** (chopped)
3 tbs dried **figs** (chopped)
1/3 cup **honey**
¼ cup **oat bran**
1 cup **oats**
1 cup low-fat **milk**
1 cup plain **yogurt**
½ cup **walnuts** (chopped)
Fresh **berries** of your choice (optional)

Makes: 5 servings
Calories: 265 per serving

Simply combine all of the ingredients in a bowl and mix together.

For maximum taste, especially on hot days, chill for 2 hours before
serving.

If desired, garnish with berries of your choice.

Enjoy!

9. Fruit and Nut Breakfast

This muesli recipe comes from Italy. It is light, yet very nutritious, combining fruits, almonds and sunflower seeds.

1 tsp **almonds**, (sliced)
¼ **mango**, (peeled, diced)
1 tsp **sunflower** seeds
½ **apple**, (cored, peeled, diced)
½ cup **oats**
1 cup low fat **milk**

Makes: 3 servings
Calories: 115 per serving

Combine the milk and oats in a bowl.

Microwave on high a setting for 2 minutes.

Remove and stir in the sunflower seeds and almond, then top with diced apple and mango.

Enjoy!

10. Salmon Omelet

Salmon is a common Mediterranean ingredient. This recipe combines it with asparagus to accompany a delicious omelet.

2 **asparagus spears**
2 **eggs**
½ tsp **extra virgin olive oil**
4 oz. (115 g) **salmon**
1 tsp low fat **milk**
2 tbs **onion** (diced)
¼ tsp **lemon juice**
½ tbs **parsley**
Sea Salt, ground **pepper, chives,** and **dill** to taste

Makes: 2 servings
Calories: 145 per serving

Heat the olive oil in a skillet over medium heat. Add the diced onion and sauté for 3 minutes, or until translucent. Add the lemon juice and asparagus, then sauté for another 2 minutes.

Combine the milk, parsley, and eggs in a bowl and beat the mixture. Season with sea salt, ground pepper, chives, and dill.

Add the mixture and salmon to the skillet. Reduce heat to low and cook for 3-5 minutes.

Fold the omelet in half, then cook for 1 more minute.

Enjoy!

11. Breakfast Smoothie

Have you ever considered making a drinkable breakfast? This healthy and tasty smoothie is an excellent alternative to traditional breakfast and also works as a quick afternoon snack.

1 **banana** (pre-sliced, frozen)
½ **ginger root** (fresh, sliced)
2 cups **baby spinach** (organic)
1 small **mango**
4-6 **ice cubes**
1/2 cup **milk** (skimmed)
1/2 cup **beet juice** (Mediterranean beet)

Makes 1- 2 servings
Calories: 175 per serving

Preheat oven to 375°F (190 °C)

Wash fresh beets under running water and dry with a kitchen towel. Brush the beets with a little olive oil, wrap in aluminum foil and bake in the oven for 50-60 minutes.

Remove from the oven and allow to cool. Once the beets are cool, peel and add one to a blender. Add the baby spinach, ginger root, banana, mango, ½ cup of milk, a couple of ice cubes and pulse until smooth.

Enjoy!

12. Oatmeal with Apples

An ideal way to start the day. It is quick and easy to prepare and very healthy.

1/3 cup **Medjool dates** (chopped, pitted)
¼ tsp **kosher salt**
½ tsp **cinnamon** (ground)
½ cup **apple** (chopped)
3 cups **water**
1 cup low fat **milk** (warmed)
1 ½ cups **quick-cooking oats**
2 tbs **almonds** (chopped)
1 tbs **honey** (optional)

Makes 4 servings
Calories: 198 per serving

Pour 3 cups of water in a pot, add the cinnamon and salt and set over high heat.
Once boiled, reduce the heat to medium-low, add oats and let cook for 3-5 minutes.

Add the almonds, chopped apples and dates. Ladle the porridge into serving bowls. If you want it sweet, sprinkle with 1 tbs honey.

Served with a glass of low-fat milk.

Enjoy!

13. Breakfast Frittata

An interesting and rich combination of smoked salmon, cream cheese and vegetables.

1 tbs **butter**
½ cup **yellow onions** (chopped)
8 oz. (230 g) **smoked salmon**, (sliced)
3 oz. (90 g) **cream cheese** (diced)
½ cup **Asiago cheese** (grated)
8 large **eggs**
½ tsp **salt**
¼ tsp **black pepper** (freshly ground)
2 tbs **fresh dill** (chopped)
1 lbs. (450 g) thin **asparagus** (trimmed, cut)
Capers for garnish (optional)

Makes 6 servings
Calories: 197 per serving

Preheat oven to 400 °F (200°C).

Place the asparagus in a pot of salted boiling water and cook for 1-2 minutes, or until tender. Drain and rinse under cold water. When completely cooled, dry with a kitchen towel and set aside.

In a deep saucepan, combine eggs, salt, ground black pepper, and cream cheese. Add the blanched asparagus and smoked salmon, then season with dill.

Melt butter in a large nonstick frying pan over medium heat. Stir in the onions and fry for 2-3 of minutes, or until tender and translucent.

Add the egg mixture to the pan, cover and let cook for about 15 minutes, or until the bottom and sides are slightly brown. Uncover, transfer the pan to the oven and bake for another 10 minutes. Sprinkle the frittata with grated cheese and bake for another 2 minutes, or until cheese has melted.

Allow the frittata to cool for a few minutes, then transfer it to a serving plate. Slice in wedges and serve with capers, if you like.

14. Mediterranean Muesli

A healthy Muesli with fruits and nuts. This breakfast needs 1-2 hours refrigeration time.

3 tbs dried **apricots** (chopped)
3 tbs **dates** (chopped, pitted)
1 cup **plain yogurt**
1 cup low-fat **milk**
1/3 cup **honey**
1 cup **regular oats**
Raspberries or other **berries** (optional)
½ cup **walnuts** (coarsely chopped)
¼ cup **oat bran**
3 tbs dried **figs** (chopped)

Makes 5 servings
Calories: 298 per serving

In a large bowl, combine the dates, dried figs, dried apricots, oat bran, honey, walnuts, and regular oats. Pour the yogurt and milk over the ingredients and mix well to combine. Refrigerate the mixture for 1-2 hours.

Divide the oat mixture among 5 serving bowls and sprinkle with berries.

Enjoy!

15. Breakfast Couscous

This breakfast has great potential for variation, because you can use whatever mix of fresh or dried fruit you prefer.

¼ cup **dried currant**
1 **cinnamon stick**
½ cup **dried apricot**
1 cup **whole wheat couscous** (uncooked)
4 tsp **butter** or **coconut butter** (melted)
¼ tsp **salt**
3 cups **soymilk**

Makes 4 servings
Calories 175 per serving

In a large pot, combine cinnamon stick and soy milk. Set over medium-high heat and cook for 3-4 minutes without letting it boil.

Remove from heat. Add the apricots, couscous, currants, and season with salt. Stir to blend. Cover and let sit for 20 minutes, then remove the cinnamon stick.

Place the couscous into 4 serving bowls. Add 1 tsp melted butter or coconut butter to each portion.

Enjoy!

16. Zucchini and Goat Cheese

A lovely dish made with fresh vegetables, milk and goat cheese.
It can be served hot or at room temperature.

2 medium **zucchinis**
2 oz. (60 g) **goat cheese** (crumbled)
8 **eggs**
1 clove **garlic** (crushed)
¼ tsp each **salt** and **pepper**
1 tbs **olive oil** or **coconut oil** (melted)
2 tbs low-fat **milk**

Makes 4 servings
Calories: 125 per serving

Preheat oven to 360°F (180°C)

Cut the zucchinis into round slices. Whisk in the eggs and milk in
a large bowl, then season with salt and pepper.

Pour the oil of your choice into an ovenproof pan and place over
medium heat. Add the crushed garlic and sliced zucchini and sauté
for 5 minutes, or until golden and just tender.

Pour the beaten eggs over the zucchini and stir-fry for 1 minute.
Sprinkle the cheese over the frittata and transfer the pan to the
oven. Bake for about 12 minutes or until the eggs are firm.

Remove from the oven and let the frittata stand for a few minutes.
Slice into 4 wedges and serve warm or at room temperature.

Enjoy!

17. Zucchini Pancakes

This moist and tasty pancake is one best ways to use zucchini for breakfast. Total preparation time is about 30 minutes.

½ cup all-purpose **flour**
6 tsp **vegetable oil** (divided)
1 cup **feta cheese** (crumbled)
4 whole **eggs** (separated)
4 cups **zucchini** (shredded)
½ cup **green onions** (finely chopped)
1 tbs fresh **mint** (chopped)
½ tsp **salt**
¼ tsp **pepper**

Makes 4 servings
Calories: 257 per serving

In a bowl, whisk the egg whites until smooth. Set aside.

In a large bowl, whip the egg yolks with flour, feta cheese, onions, zucchini, mint, salt and pepper. Add the egg whites, fold to blend.

In a large pan, heat 2 teaspoons of oil over medium heat and fry 1/3 cupful of batter for about 2 minutes on each side, or until golden brown. Repeat for the rest of the batter.

Enjoy!

18. Quinoa with Vanilla

Healthy almond quinoa with apricots, dates, honey and cinnamon is the best way to start your day.

1 tsp **vanilla extract**
1 tsp **cinnamon** (ground)
1 cup **quinoa**
2 tbs **honey**
2 **dates** (pitted, chopped)
5 **apricots** (finely chopped)
¼ cup raw **almonds** (chopped)
2 cups **milk**
1/3 tsp **salt**

Makes 4 servings
Calories: 235 per serving

Place the almonds in a pan and toast over medium heat for 4 to 5 minutes, or until golden and fragrant. Remove from heat and set aside.

Combine the quinoa and cinnamon in a pot over medium heat. Stir in the milk and salt, then bring the mixture to a boil. Reduce heat to low, cover and let the dish simmer for 15 minutes.

Add the honey, apricots, vanilla, dates, and half the almonds into the pot. Stir to combine. Garnish the quinoa with the remaining almonds and serve.

Enjoy!

19. Pasta with Spinach and Raisins

Pasta is not only good for lunch or dinner, it can be a wholesome breakfast as well!

8 oz. (230 g) **farfalle pasta**
2 tbs **olive oil** or **coconut oil**
4 **garlic cloves** (crushed)
20 oz. (570 g) **garbanzos**
½ cup unsalted **chicken broth**
½ cup **golden raisins**
4 cups **fresh spinach** (chopped)
2 tbs **Parmesan cheese**
Black peppercorns (cracked to taste)

Makes 7 servings
Calories: 295 per serving

Cook the pasta according to package instructions until it is al dente.

Place the oil of your choice in a large saucepan over medium heat. Add the garlic and sauté for 1 minute, then add the garbanzos and chicken broth. Stir to mix.

Once the mixture is heated through, stir in the spinach and the raisins. Cook for 3-4 minutes, or until spinach wilts. Divide the sauce into 7 portions.

Place the pasta on serving plates. Top with a portion of spinach mixture, sprinkle with parmesan cheese and peppercorns to taste.

Enjoy!

20. Mediterranean Strata

This is an elaborate recipe for a Sunday brunch. It combines French baguette, spinach and plum tomatoes with Asiago and feta cheese. At best, prepare this dish one day prior to serving, so it can chill overnight before the final baking process.

1 tbs **arrowroot flour**
Olive oil or **coconut oil**
7-oz. (200 g) **baby spinach**
1 lb. (450 g) **plum tomato** (sliced)
2 loaves **French bread baguette** (sliced)
4 oz. (115 g) **feta cheese** (crumbled)
3 oz. (85 g) **Asiago cheese** (grated)
18 oz. (230 g) **mushrooms** (sliced)
3 cups low-fat **milk**
2 tbs **Dijon mustard**
1 ½ tsp **oregano** (dried)
4 **garlic cloves** (minced)
5 large **eggs** (lightly beaten)
4 large **egg whites** (lightly beaten)
1 cup **onion** (chopped)
½ tsp each **salt** and **black pepper**

Makes 10 servings
Calories: 297 per serving

Preheat oven to 350°F (180 °C).

Arrange French bread slices on a baking tray and bake for 10-12 minutes, or until lightly toasted.

Heat the oil of your choice in large frying pan over medium-high heat. Stir in the garlic, onion, and mushrooms. Cook 5 minutes, or until softened. Sprinkle 1 tbs arrowroot flour over the vegetables and stir-fry for 1 more minute.

Add the spinach and cook for about 4 minutes, or until spinach wilts. Season with ¼ tsp salt and ¼ tsp pepper, then remove the mixture from the heat.

Coat a baking dish with the oil of your choice and arrange half the bread slices on it. Top with the spinach mixture, followed by the tomato slices. Sprinkle with feta and half of the Asiago cheese, then place the remaining bread slices on top.

In a small bowl, mix together milk, salt and pepper, Dijon mustard, oregano, egg whites and eggs until smooth. Pour the mixture over bread and top with remaining Asiago cheese. Chill the strata for 6 hours.

Heat the oven to 350°F (180 °C).

Bake the strata for 35 minutes, or until the eggs are cooked through and the edges of the strata have slightly browned. Remove from the oven, cut into wedges and serve immediately.

Enjoy!

21. Lemon Scones

Twenty minutes and these wonderful lemon scones are ready to be served. They taste great and work well with a cup of tea or coffee.

2 ¼ cup **arrowroot flour**
½ tsp **baking soda**
½ tsp **salt**
¼ cup **butter** or **coconut butter**
1 **lemon zest**
2 tsp **lemon juice**
¾ cup **buttermilk**

Makes 12 servings
Calories 163 per serving

Preheat the oven to 400°F (200°C).

Combine 2 cups of flour, baking soda, and salt in a medium bowl. Stir to mix. Add the butter of your choice and beat until the mixture turns to fine crumbs. Stir in the buttermilk and lemon zest.

Coat your working surface with the remaining flour and place the dough on it. Form the dough into a ball and flatten it into a circle, using a rolling pin. Divide into 4 pieces, then slice each part into 3 smaller wedges for a total of 12 scones.

Arrange the scones on a greased baking sheet and bake for about 13 minutes, or until golden brown. Sprinkle the lemon juice over the scones and serve.

Enjoy!

22. Potato Omelet

This is a Spanish dish that can be served as breakfast or light lunch.

1 small **onion** (thinly sliced)
3 tsp **olive oil** or **coconut oil**
3 cups **baby spinach** (roughly chopped)
½ tsp **paprika**
1 cup **red potatoes** (diced)
6 large **eggs**
4 large **egg whites**
1 tbs **thyme** (chopped)
½ cup **Jack cheese** (shredded)
½ tsp each **salt** and **pepper**

Makes 6 servings
Calories: 167 per serving

Heat 2 tsp of your chosen oil in a frying pan over medium heat. Add the onion and sauté for about 3 minutes, or until golden and fragrant. Stir in the potatoes, paprika and thyme and sauté for about 3 more of minutes.

In a large bowl, combine the eggs and egg whites and lightly beat with a whisk. Add the potato mixture, spinach and cheese, then season with salt and pepper. Stir to combine.

Rinse the pan and set over medium heat, adding the remaining 1 tsp oil. Once hot, pour in the egg mixture, cover and cook for 5 minutes, or until the edges are set and the bottom has browned.

Flip with a wooden spatula and cook for another 5 minutes to brown the other side. Transfer to a serving plate and serve.

Enjoy!

Lunch Recipes

1. Classic Chicken Salad

This salad includes a generous amount of chicken, red onion marinated in red wine vinegar, capers, olives, and extra virgin olive oil. You can eat it as is, or serve it in lettuce cups.

4 tbs **parsley leaves** (chopped)
1 tbs **basil leaves** (chopped)
1 tbs **oregano leaves** (chopped)
1 tsp **chili flakes**
1 ½ cups **olives** (pitted, chopped)
2 tbs **capers**
4 tbs **extra virgin olive oil**
2 lbs. (900 g) skinless, boneless **chicken breasts** (shredded)
4 tbs **red wine vinegar**
1 cup **red onions** (chopped)
Salt and **black pepper** (ground)

Makes: 8 servings
Calories: 125 per serving

Rinse the chicken breasts (make sure they are skinless and boneless) well and pat dry with paper towels. Shred into small pieces. Set aside.

In a medium-sized bowl, combine chopped onions with the red wine vinegar. Stir well and set aside to allow the red onions to absorb the vinegar's flavor.

Meanwhile, put enough water and a bit of salt in a large saucepan and bring it to a boil. Slice the chicken breasts in half. Transfer them to the saucepan once the water has started boiling. Reduce to very low heat and allow the chicken breasts to simmer for 10 to 15 minutes, until fully cooked.

While the chicken is simmering, combine the chopped oregano leaves, basil leaves, chili flakes, olives, capers, and extra virgin olive oil in a large bowl. Stir well until thoroughly combined. Set aside.

When the chicken is cooked, transfer on a chopping board and allow it to cool. Meanwhile, add in the marinated red onions to the bowl containing the oregano and olives. Mix well.

When the chicken is cool enough, cut it into shreds, then add into the olive mixture. Stir well to combine.

Add the chopped parsley into the chicken and olive mixture, then stir again until well combined. Season with table salt and freshly ground black pepper.

Serve immediately, or let it cool to room temperature before serving.

Enjoy!

2. Classic Mediterranean Pizza

This pizza recipe features classic Mediterranean flavors like olives, feta cheese, oregano, zucchini, and tomatoes. It is a great, healthy alternative to traditional pizzas but just as delicious.

½ cup pitted **black olives** (chopped)
8 oz. (230 g) **feta cheese** (crumbled)
½ tsp dried **oregano** or 2 tbs **oregano leaves** (chopped)
1 **zucchini** (sliced thinly)
14.5 oz. (410 g) canned **tomatoes** (diced)
1 lb. (450 g) **pizza dough** (frozen)
2 tbs extra virgin **olive oil**

Makes: 8 servings
Calories: 270 per serving

Preheat the oven to 475F (250°C). Use 1 tbs of olive oil to grease the bottom and sides of a baking pan.

Transfer the pizza dough (thawed) to the baking pan, roll it out and evenly spread it across the pan. If the pizza dough is too firm at first, let it stand for a couple of minutes before proceeding.

Add the diced tomatoes and spread across the pizza dough. Arrange the slices of zucchini on top of the diced tomatoes.

Top the zucchini slices with the dried oregano or chopped fresh oregano leaves.

Crumble the feta cheese on top of the pizza. Add in the pitted olives last and spread evenly across the pizza.

Bake the pizza in the oven for 15 to 20 minutes, or until the cheese is browned lightly, and the crust has become golden brown. To check for the crust, use a spatula to lift up the pizza.

Remove the pizza from the oven and drizzle the remaining 1 tbs extra virgin olive oil evenly across the top.

Let the pizza rest for 5 minutes before cutting and serving.

3. Mediterranean Potato Pancakes

Potato pancakes are traditionally eaten during the Hanukkah, a
Jewish holiday, but a lot of people eat them any time of the year
because they really have a year-round appeal. This recipe for
potato pancakes is made more exciting with the inclusion of flour
made from chickpeas, and a lot of spices and herbs.

½ tsp **turmeric powder** or **turmeric** (ground)
1 ½ tsp **cumin seeds**
3 tbs extra virgin **olive oil**
¼ tsp **cayenne pepper**
½ tsp **black pepper** (ground)
1 ½ tsp **table salt**
2 tsp **coriander** (ground)
1 ½ tbs **jalapeño** (seeds removed, minced)
2 large **eggs**
½ cup **chickpea flour**
½ cup **cilantro leaves** (chopped)
½ cup **spring onions** (finely chopped)
1 large **white onion** (grated)
2 ½ lbs. (1,15 kg) **white potatoes** (grated)

Makes: 18 servings
Calories: 83 per serving

Peel the potatoes and grate them. Transfer to a large enough bowl
and pour in enough cold water to submerge the potatoes. Set
aside.

Beat the eggs in a small bowl and set aside.

Transfer the grated onion and grated potatoes in a large colander
and drain thoroughly. Mix them well. Then, using your bare
hands, squeeze the potato and onion mixture to wheedle out as
much liquids as possible.

Transfer the potato and onion mixture to a large mixing bowl. Add
in the chopped spring onions and stir well.

Add in the cayenne pepper, ground black pepper, table salt,
ground coriander, minced jalapeño, beaten eggs, chickpea flour,

and chopped cilantro leaves. Stir everything together until well combined.

In a large skillet, heat 2 tbs extra virgin olive oil. Add in the turmeric powder and cumin seeds and sauté for about 30 seconds, stirring constantly. Transfer the turmeric and cumin mixture into the potato mixture. Cover with a lid and let the flavors infuse for about 30 minutes.

Meanwhile, preheat the oven to 250F (120°C). Heat the remaining 1 tbs of extra virgin olive oil in the same skillet you used for the turmeric and cumin seeds. Add 3 tbs of the infused potato mixture to the skillet for each potato pancake and flatten it to roughly 4-inch (10 cm) rounds using a spatula. Cook for 5 minutes per side, or until golden.

Transfer the potato pancakes to a baking dish and keep them warm in the oven. Continue cooking the potato pancakes in the skillet, adding more extra virgin olive oil if needed.

Serve the potato pancakes immediately.

Enjoy!

4. Greek Shrimp Pasta

Shrimp pasta it is colorful, fresh, and very flavorful. You can use any type of pasta for it.

¼ cup **feta cheese**
8 oz. (225 g) uncooked **pasta**
¼ tsp **black pepper** (ground)
2 tbs **capers**
1/3 cup pitted **Kalamata olives** (chopped)
¼ **fresh basil leaves** (chopped)
2 cups **plum tomatoes** (diced)
1 lb. (450 g) **shrimp** (peeled)
2 **cloves of garlic** (crushed, minced)
3 tsp **extra virgin olive oil**

Makes: 4 servings
Calories: 204 per serving

Cook the pasta according to packaging instructions. Drain in a colander and set aside.

In a large skillet, heat the olive oil over medium heat. Add the minced garlic and cook for about 30 seconds. Add the shrimp and sauté for 1 more minute.

Add the chopped basil leaves and the diced plum tomatoes. Reduce to low heat and allow to simmer for 3 minutes, or until the tomatoes are soft. Add the black pepper, capers, and Kalamata olives. Stir well to combine.

Transfer the shrimp mixture to the saucepan containing the cooked pasta. Toss everything together until thoroughly combined.

Divide the shrimp pasta equally between four individual serving bowls. Top with crumbled feta cheese and serve.

Enjoy!

5. Mediterranean Pita Bread with Hummus

Hummus is a classic Middle Eastern delicacy that is usually used as a dip and served with pita bread. It is made from pureed chickpeas and tahini, a special kind of sesame paste. This recipe is very easy to prepare and great for the Mediterranean diet!

4 **pepperoncini peppers** (sliced thinly)
2 large **plum tomatoes** (sliced thinly)
2 small **cucumbers** (sliced thinly)
4 tbs **feta cheese** (crumbled)
4 6-inch (15 cm) whole-wheat round **pita bread**
1 cup **hummus** with **roasted peppers**

Makes: 4 servings
Calories: 310 per serving

Cut the pita bread rounds in half. Spread 2 tbs of hummus on each pit bread half.

Crumble feta cheese equally between the 8 pita bread halves.

Arrange the slices of tomatoes and cucumbers on top of the pita bread halves.

Top with slices of pepperoncini peppers.

Serve immediately and enjoy!

6. Pasta Coconut Salad

As mentioned in section 1, coconut products are extremely healthy and make a great addition to the Mediterranean diet. This recipe makes use of this ingredient. It can either be seen as a meal or noodle salad, depending on whether you refrigerate it at the end or eat it warm.

4 tbs **coconut oil**
2-3 cloves **garlic**, minced
Shredded **coconut**
½ cup **red onion** (diced)
¼ cup **yellow bell pepper** (diced)
¼ cup **green bell pepper** (diced)
¼ cup **red bell pepper** (diced)
1 lb. **penne pasta** (cooked)
¼ cup **sun dried tomatoes** in **olive oil** (chopped)
½ cup **basil** (chopped)
Salt and **pepper** (optional)
Parmesan cheese (grated, optional)

Makes: 4 servings
Calories: 255 per serving

Make sure you have the pasta cooked by the end, so either cook it first or do it at the same time.

Melt the coconut oil in a medium sized frying pan. Combine garlic, onion, all peppers, and basil in the pan, then stir them together. Cook until tender.

Transfer the mix from the pan to the cooked pasta. Add the sun dried tomatoes and stir.
Optionally, season with salt and pepper and top with parmesan cheese.

Top with shredded coconut and serve.

Enjoy!

7. Stuffed Bell Peppers

Recipes of this kind are interesting, delicious and nutritious at the same time. Peppers are the perfect vessels to combine many ingredients.

3 **red bell peppers**
1 lb. (450 g) **lean beef** (ground)
1 **egg** (lightly beaten)
28 oz. (800 g) low-sodium stewed **tomatoes** (chopped)
1/3 cup **feta cheese** (crumbled)
10 oz. (280 g) frozen **spinach**
½ cup **bulgur**
1 medium **zucchini**, (coarsely grated)
1 small **onion** (minced)
½tsp dried **oregano**
½ tsp **salt** and
¼ tsp **black pepper** (ground)

Makes: 6 servings
Calories: 225 per serving

Preheat the oven to 350F (180°C)
Combine the spinach, onion, zucchini, beef, bulgur, oregano, salt, black pepper, and egg in a bowl.

Cut the bell peppers in half lengthwise, then remove the cores and ribs. Place the halves on a baking dish and fill with the mixture from the bowl. Add the chopped tomatoes to the bell peppers and top with feta cheese.

Cover with foil and bake for 35 minutes. Uncover and continue cooking for another 20 minutes, until the peppers are tender.

Serve and enjoy!

8. Tomato Soup

This is my standard recipe for tomato soup. It is perfect for lunch or as entry for dinner and has a great taste whether it is served hot or cold.

28 oz. (800 g) **tomatoes** (cored)
½ **onion**, (chopped)
2 cups **vegetable broth**
½ cup **white wine**
2 tbs **tomato paste**
2 tsp **dried basil**
½ tsp **cumin** (ground)
2/3 cup low fat **milk**
1 tsp **salt**
¼ tsp **black pepper** (ground)

Makes 5 servings
Calories: 150 per serving

Place all ingredients except the milk in a slow cooker. Cover, set to low heat and cook for 4 hours.

Remove and add to a blender. Let it cool for 30 minutes. When cooled, blend completely.

Pour into a saucepan and add the milk. Heat it up, but don't boil it.

Optionally, serve with crackers or croutons.

Enjoy!

9. Mediterranean Lamb Pilaf

A nutritious lamb meal with rice and a touch of mint and lemon flavors.

¾ lb. (340 g) lean **lamb** (ground)
1 large **onion** (chopped)
14 oz. (400 g) fat-free **chicken broth**
1 **plum tomato** (chopped)
3 **garlic** cloves (minced)
1 **carrot** (chopped)
1 cup uncooked **rice**
2 tbs **mint** (chopped)
3 tbs **lemon juice**
¼ tsp **cinnamon** (ground)
¼ cup **flat-leaf parsley** (chopped, divided)
¾ tsp **salt**

Makes 4 servings
Calories: 375 per serving

Place the onion, garlic, carrot and lamb in a skillet over medium heat. Cook for 5 minutes while stirring to crumble the meat.

Add the cinnamon and rice, stir and sauté for 3 minutes. Add the chicken broth, then bring to a boil. Cover, reduce the heat and simmer for 25 minutes, or until all liquid is absorbed.

Remove from heat and add the tomato, parsley, salt, mint and lemon juice. Stir to mix, cover and let it sit for 5 minutes.

Serve and enjoy!

10. Ratatouille

Ratatouille is a delicious vegetable stew that originated in France. This version is prepared in a frying pan and works very well with pasta.

1 lb. (450 g) **bell peppers**, (stemmed, seeded, diced)
28 oz. (800 g) **tomatoes** (diced)
8 oz. (225 g) **eggplant** (diced)
8 oz. (225 g) **zucchini** (diced)
8 oz. (225 g) **yellow summer squash** (diced)
8 oz. (225 g) **onion** (peeled, diced)
3 tbs **extra virgin olive oil**
2 **garlic** cloves (peeled, minced)
¾ cup **basil leaves** (chopped)
½ tsp **salt**
¼ tsp **pepper**

Makes 4 servings
Calories: 220 per serving

Heat 1 ½ tbs olive oil in a frying pan over medium heat. Add garlic and onion, then sauté for 5 minutes while stirring, until onion is translucent.

Add the eggplant, salt, tomatoes, pepper, and ½ cup water to the pan. Cover, reduce heat and simmer for 10 minutes, or until the eggplant is soft. Keep stirring occasionally.

Add the bell peppers, yellow squash, and zucchini. Cover and cook for another 10 minutes, or until the squash is tender.

Add the remaining 1 ½ tbs olive oil and basil. If needed, add more salt and peppers to taste.

Serve with pasta and enjoy!

11. Greek Chicken Salad

A flavorful Greek salad with chicken, spinach and chickpeas.

1 lb. (450 g) **chicken breast** (skinless, boneless)
7 oz. (200 g) **baby spinach**
15 oz. (425 g) **chickpeas**
¼ cup **chicken broth** (fat-free, less-sodium)
½ tsp **lemon rind** (grated)
1 tbs fresh **lemon juice**
1 tbs **balsamic vinegar**
1 tsp **garlic** (bottled, minced)
1 tsp **Dijon mustard**
1 tsp **olive oil**
1 ½ cups **red onion** (chopped)
1 ¼ cups **yellow bell pepper** (chopped)
2 oz. (60 g) **feta cheese** (crumbled)
½ tsp **salt** + ¼ tsp **black pepper**
Cooking spray

Makes 4 servings
Calories: 315 per serving

In a small bowl, combine the lemon rind, juice, balsamic vinegar, garlic, Dijon mustard, chicken broth, olive oil, and salt. Set aside.

Heat olive oil in a large saucepan over medium-high heat. Season chicken with black pepper, then place in the pan and sauté for 4 minutes.

Turn the chicken to fry the other side. Add onion and sauté for about 3 minutes, or until chicken is brown and onion has softened.

Transfer to a cutting board to cool. Thinly slice the chicken and place in a large bowl, then add the chickpeas, bell pepper, spinach, and feta cheese. Pour the prepared vinaigrette over salad and mix gently to combine.

Enjoy!

12. Greek Veggie Salad

This is a fantastic, plain salad recipe that features classic ingredients for Greek salad. It is quick and easy to make and very refreshing.

3 cups **tomato** (diced)
3 tbs **dill** (chopped)
1 tbs **olive oil**
1 tbs **lemon juice**
1 tsp **oregano** (dried)
¼ cup **parsley** (chopped)
6 cups **Romaine lettuce** (shredded)
1 cup **red onion** (thinly sliced)
3 oz. (85 g) **feta cheese** (crumbled)
3 **whole wheat pitas** (quartered)
1 tbs **capers**
18 oz. (510 g) **chickpeas** (drained, rinsed)
1 **cucumber** (peeled, sliced)

Makes 6 servings
Calories: 312 per serving

For the dressing, combine the olive oil, dill, parsley, and oregano in a cup. Mix to combine.

In a large bowl, combine the lettuce, red onion, capers, feta cheese, cucumber and tomatoes. Pour the prepared dressing over the salad. Stir to coat.

Serve with 2 pita quarters per serving.

Enjoy!

13. Linguine and clams

If you like garlic you will love this dish. It combines garlic, basil, and red pepper flavors.

1 cup **green peas** (frozen)
2 tbs **olive oil**
1 ½ tsp **garlic** (minced)
1 cup **vegetable broth**
¼ tsp **red pepper** (crushed)
2 oz. (60 g) **Parmesan cheese** (shredded)
9 oz. (250 g) **linguine**
6 oz. (170 g) **clams** (chopped)
2 tbs fresh **basil** (chopped)
¼ cup dry **white wine**

Makes 4 servings
Calories: 295 per serving

Place the pasta in a pot of boiling water and cook according to package instructions. Drain in a colander and keep covered.

Heat oil in a large nonstick frying pan over medium-high heat. Add the garlic and sauté fry for 1 minute.

Drain clams, reserving ½ cup of juice. Add the broth, reserved clam juice, and wine to the garlic. Season with pepper and bring to a boil.

Once boiling, decrease heat and simmer for 5 minutes, stirring occasionally. Stir in the clams and peas. Cook for another 3-4 minutes, or until heated through.

Add the cooked pasta and gently stir to coat. Remove to a serving platter and sprinkle with basil and cheese.

Enjoy!

14. Pita Salad

This salad is one of my favorites to serve at parties. The fennel adds a nice crisp texture to it.

¼ cup **red onion** (sliced)
2 cups **fennel bulb** (sliced)
½ **cucumber** (halved, sliced)
½ tsp **oregano** (chopped)
2 **pitas breads**
1 tbs **white wine vinegar**
½ tsp **salt** (divided)
¼ tsp **black pepper** (divided)
¼ cup fresh **lemon juice**
3 tbs **olive oil**
1 cup boneless **chicken breast** (shredded)
½ cup **flat-leaf parsley** (chopped)

Makes 4 servings
Calories: 234 per serving

Preheat oven to 350°F (175°C)

Place pitas on a baking tray and bake for about 10 minutes, or until toasted. Remove from the oven and allow to cool for a couple of minutes. Tear pitas into small pieces and place in a bowl.

Add the fennel, chicken, red onion, and cucumber to the pitas. Sprinkle with chopped parsley and season with ¼ tsp salt and 1/8 tsp pepper.

In a small bowl, combine lemon juice, oregano, vinegar, and the remaining salt and pepper, then add the olive oil and mix well. Pour the mixture over the salad and stir to coat.

Enjoy!

15. Stuffed Tomatoes

A fabulous party dish that most of my guests crave for. The Kalamata olives work really well with tomatoes and goat cheese.

2 large **tomatoes**
½ cup **garlic croutons**
1 oz. (30 g) **goat cheese** (crumbled)
¼ cup **Kalamata olives** (sliced, pitted)
2 tbs **vinaigrette** or **Italian dressing**
2 tbs **thyme** or **basil** (chopped)

Makes: 4 servings
Calories: 95 per serving

Preheat broiler.

Halve the tomatoes and discard seeds with a teaspoon. Cut out the pulp and chop it, then place it in a bowl.

Add the goat cheese, olives, croutons, thyme and dressing to the bowl. Stir to combine. Fill the mixture into the tomatoes.

Transfer the stuffed tomatoes to a baking tray or broiler pan and broil for about 5 minutes, or until heated through and the cheese has melted

Enjoy!

16. Chorizo with Rice

This is a spicy, aromatic dish with basmati rice and Mediterranean flavors. You can substitute chorizo with spicy lamb, chicken or Italian sausages.

9 oz. (250 g) **chorizo** (sliced)
4 **garlic cloves** (crushed)
1 tsp **paprika** (smoked)
14 oz. (400 g) can **tomatoes** (chopped)
9 oz. (250 g) **basmati rice**
1 tbs **olive oil**
1 large **onion** (thinly sliced)
1 cup **stock**
1 **lemon**
2 **bay leaves**
1 small **bunch parsley** (chopped)

Makes 4 servings
Calories: 355 per serving

Heat the oil in an iron-cast pot over medium-high heat. Stir in the onion and sauté for about 5 minutes, or until tender and translucent.

Move the onion to the side of the pot and add the chorizo. Cook for a few minutes until lightly browned.

Now stir in the paprika, tomatoes, and garlic. Bring the mixture to a boil and cook for about 5 minutes. Add the rice, lemon zest, bay leaves, and stock. Stir, cover and bring to a simmer over low heat. Cook for about 11 minutes.

Remove from heat and allow to cook for 10 minutes before serving. Serve with lemon wedges and garnish with parsley.

Enjoy!

17. Grilled Sandwich

A delicious sandwich recipe with eggplant and mozzarella.

1 large **eggplant** (cut into rounds)
½ cup **mozzarella cheese** (shredded)
1 cup **tomatoes** (fire-roasted, crushed)
3 tbs **basil** (chopped, divided)
3 tbs **Parmesan** (finely shredded)
4 small pieces **focaccia bread**
2 tsp **olive oil**
5 oz. (140 g) **baby spinach**
¼ tsp **salt**

Makes 4 servings
Calories: 145 per serving

Preheat grill to medium-high heat.
Arrange eggplant rounds on a baking tray and season with salt.
Lightly coat both sides of the eggplants with olive oil.

In a small bowl, mix together the shredded Parmesan and Mozzarella. Brush both sides of the focaccia bread with oil.

Place the fresh spinach in a microwave-safe bowl and microwave on high setting for 3 minutes, or until wilted. Remove and combine tomatoes and 2 tbs of basil in another microwave-safe bowl, then microwave for 2 minutes.

Grill the bread for 1 minute on each side, or until toasted. Transfer the eggplant and bread to a baking tray. Reduce grill heat to medium.

Top each slice of bread with e 1 eggplant round, followed by 1 tbs tomatoes, 1 tbs spinach and 1 tbs cheese. Garnish with fresh basil. Place the baking tray on the grill for about 6 minutes, or until sandwiches are heated through and the cheese is melted.

Enjoy!

18. Mediterranean Pasta

This pasta recipe with eggplant, olives and tomato sauce makes even kids want to eat their veggies!

1 medium **eggplant** (cut)
12 oz. (340 g) **whole-wheat pasta**
4 **plum tomatoes** (diced)
¼ cup **parsley** or **basil** (chopped)
4 tsp **capers**
2 **cloves garlic** (minced)
2 tbs **red-wine vinegar**
1/3 cup **green olives** (chopped pitted)
2 tbs **olive oil**
¾ tsp **salt**
½ tsp **pepper** (ground)

Makes: 5 servings
Per serving: 235 calories

Start with making the sauce. Heat oil in a large frying pan over medium heat. Add the eggplant and sauté for about 5 minutes, stirring occasionally.

Stir in the garlic and sauté for about 1 minute, or until golden and fragrant. Add olives, tomatoes, capers. Add the vinegar and season with salt and pepper. Continue cooking for about 6 minutes, stirring occasionally.

Meanwhile, place the pasta in a pot of boiling water and cook according to package directions. Transfer to a colander to drain.

Place the cooked pasta on a serving dish, top with the sauce, and garnish with parsley or basil.

Serve and enjoy!

19. Pasta with shrimps and olives

The ingredients of this dish are a bit surprising but come together really well. The whole process will take you no longer than 20 minutes.

1 lb. (450 g) **shrimps** (peeled, deveined)
2 oz. (60 g) **feta cheese** (crumbled)
1/3 cup **Kalamata olives** (chopped, pitted)
¼ cup **fresh basil** (thinly sliced)
2 cups **plum tomato** (chopped)
2 tsp **olive oil**
¼ tsp **black pepper** (freshly ground)
2 **garlic cloves** (minced)
2 tbs **capers** (drained)
4 cups cooked **pasta**

Makes 4 servings
Calories: 356 per serving

Heat the olive oil in a large frying pan over medium-high heat. Add the minced garlic and sauté for a few seconds, then add the shrimps and sauté for 1 minute.

Add the basil and tomato, then cook for about 4 minutes, or until tomato is tender. Add the capers and Kalamata olives and season the mixture with black pepper. Stir to combine.

In a large bowl, combine the cooked pasta and shrimp mixture. Toss to coat and sprinkle with cheese.

Enjoy!

20. Feta-Mint Lamb

These meatballs go great with rice or warmed pita bread.

1 tbs **fresh mint** (chopped)
2 large **garlic cloves** (pressed)
1/3 cup **feta cheese** (crumbled)
1 ½ lbs. (700 g) **lamb shoulder** (ground)
1 tbs **olive oil** or **coconut oil**
1 ½ tsp **salt**

Makes 10 servings
Calories 252 per serving

In a cup, mix the feta and mint. Set aside.

In a large bowl, combine the ground lamb and garlic, then season with salt. Form the mixture into 10 balls. Make a hole in each ball with your finger and fill with 1 tsp feta-mint mixture. Close the holes so the filling stays in the center of each ball.

Heat olive oil in a pan over medium heat. Add the meatballs and fry until golden-brown on all sides.

Serve with rice or warmed pita bread.

Enjoy!

21. Portobello with Filling

Portobello mushrooms make wonderful mini casseroles. In this recipe, we stuff them with carrot, onion, and red and green pepper. Serve them with couscous, rice, or a mixed salad.
The Portobello caps need to be 4-5 inches (10-13 cm) in diameter.

2 oz. (60 g) **feta cheese** (crumbled)
¼ cup **carrots** (chopped)
¼ cup **red bell pepper** (chopped)
4 **Portobello caps** (4-5 inches each)
¼ tsp **Italian seasoning** (dried)
4 tsp **Parmesan cheese** (grated)
3 cups **French bread** (cubed, toasted)
¼ cup **green bell pepper** (chopped)
¼ cup **celery** (chopped)
¼ cup **onion** (chopped)
3 tbs **balsamic vinaigrette** (divided)
½ cup **vegetable broth**
4 cups **mixed salad greens**
¼ tsp **black pepper**
Cooking spray
2 **garlic cloves** (minced)

Makes 4 servings
Calories: 175 per serving

Preheat oven to 350°F (180°C).

Remove stems from mushrooms, then cut stems to fill ¼ cup. Discard or preserve the remaining stems.

In a medium bowl, combine onion, carrot, celery, both bell peppers, garlic, and chopped stems. Season with Italian seasoning and mix.

Heat olive oil in a large pan over medium heat. Add the vegetable mixture to the pan and cook for about 10 minutes, or until vegetables begin to soften.

Transfer to a large bowl. Add toasted bread, broth, and feta cheese. Toss to coat.

With a spoon, remove brown gills from the undersides of the caps and discard. Coat a baking sheet with cooking spray and place caps on it, stems pointing up. Brush all caps with 1 tbs vinaigrette.

Sprinkle with parmesan cheese and ground black pepper. Fill the underside of each mushroom with bread-feta-broth mixture. Bake in the oven for about 20 minutes, or until mushrooms are softened.

Combine salad greens and 2 tbs vinaigrette in a bowl, then toss to coat. For each serving, place 1 cup of salad and 1 mushroom on a plate.

Enjoy!

22. Fish Fillets

This seafood dish is a big winner not only for lunch but on parties as well. It is best served with rice.

4 **tilapia fillets** (7 oz. / 200 g each)
¼ cup **arrowroot flour**
2 tbs **olive oil** or **coconut oil**
3 tbs **butter** or **coconut butter**
½ cup **white wine**
¼ cup **lemon juice**
2 tbs **fresh parsley** (finely chopped)
1 tbs **capers**
Salt

Makes 4 servings
Calories: 275 per serving

Season the fish slightly with salt and coat with flour on all sides.

Heat 1 tbs each oil and butter in a griddle over medium-high heat, until butter is melted. Add 2 fillets to the griddle and sauté for about 4 minutes, or until a golden crust forms on both sides.

Transfer to a plate and cover with aluminum foil to stay warm. Add 1 more tbs of oil to the pan and fry the 2 remaining fillets.

In a pot, combine the lemon juice and wine and bring to a boil. Remove from heat. Add fillets, capers, parsley and the remaining butter. Stir until butter melts.

Place fillets on 4 serving plates and top with the sauce. It is best served with rice.

Enjoy!

Snack Recipes

1. Marinated Feta Cheese and Olives

Feta cheese and olives marinated with garlic, lemon, and rosemary are amazing together with warm crusty bread slices.

1 **warm crusty bread** such as baguette (sliced)
½ tsp **black pepper** (ground)
1 pinch of **red peppers** (crushed)
1 tsp **fresh rosemary leaves** (chopped)
2 **garlic cloves** (minced finely)
Juice of ½ **lemon**
Zest of ½ **lemon**
Grated rind of 1 lemon
2 tbs extra virgin **olive oil**
½ cup **feta cheese** (diced)
1 cup pitted **Kalamata olives** (sliced)

Makes: 2 servings
Calories: 102 per serving

In a large mixing bowl, combine the freshly ground black pepper, crushed red peppers, chopped rosemary leaves, minced garlic, lemon juice, and lemon zest. Mix well.

Add the diced feta cheese and the halved pitted Kalamata olives. Stir well until combined. Let the flavors infuse for 5 minutes.

Serve with the slices of warm crusty bread.

You can prepare this ahead of time and refrigerate it for up to 24 hours.

Enjoy!

2. Olives and Tomatoes with Cheese Picnic

This recipe combines tangy cheese, salty olives, and sweet tomatoes. It is great as a snack or for picnics and can be prepared in just ten minutes or less!

6 **olives**
¼ oz. (7 g) **aged cheese** (sliced thinly)
10 **cherry tomatoes**
1 loaf **whole wheat crusty bread**

Makes: 2 servings
Calories: 104 calories per serving

Slice the olives and tomatoes in half. Set aside.

Cut the crusty bread into bit-size pieces.

Slice the cheese thinly.

Combine all ingredients in a portable container.

Enjoy!

3. Paprika Hard-Boiled Eggs

Paprika is a great ingredient to make hardboiled eggs more interesting and healthier at the same time.

1 tsp **paprika powder**
1 tsp **kosher salt**
2 tsp extra virgin **olive oil**
8 **hardboiled eggs** (sliced in half)

Makes: 8 servings
Calories: 85 per serving

Slice the hardboiled eggs in half

Dip each half in extra virgin olive oil.

Sprinkle with a bit of paprika powder and kosher salt.

Serve immediately.

Enjoy during snack time!

4. Lemon Cream with Berries

Combining reduced-fat cream cheese with Greek yogurt creates a delicious mixture. Top it with berries of your choice. I recommend raspberries or blueberries for this.

2 cups **fresh berries** of your choice
2 tsp **lemon rind** (freshly grated)
1 tsp organic **honey**
¾ cup plain **Greek yogurt** or low-fat **vanilla yogurt**
4 oz. (115 g) reduced-fat **cream cheese**

Makes: 4 servings
Calories: 151 per serving

In a medium-sized bowl, break the cream cheese apart using a fork.

Add in the organic honey and the Greek yogurt or vanilla yogurt and beat everything together using a handheld electric mixer at high speed until the mixture is creamy and smooth. Stir in the freshly grated lemon rind.

Prepare 4 wine glasses or dessert dishes, and add a bit of lemon cream cheese mixture on each. Top with a layer of berries. Then, add another layer of lemon cream cheese mixture. Keep layering alternately until everything has been used up. Serve immediately.

You can cover the lemon cream cheese mixture and store it in the refrigerator for up to eight hours if you are not serving it immediately.

Enjoy!

5. Fruit Couscous Salad

Couscous is a classic whole wheat dish usually served with meat, but is great with fruit salad too!

2 tbs **almonds** (toasted, chopped)
½ cup **raspberries**
½ cup **blueberries**
1 cup **nectarine** (chopped)
2 cups 100% **whole-wheat couscous** (cooked)
¼ tsp **ground black pepper**
¼ tsp **table salt**
2 tsp **shallots** (chopped)
1 tbs **apple cider vinegar**
2 tbs **orange juice**
2 tbs **extra virgin olive oil**

Makes: 4 servings
Calories: 244 per serving

In a large mixing bowl, whisk together the apple cider vinegar, ground black pepper, table salt, shallots, orange juice, and extra virgin olive oil.

Add in the cooked couscous and stir well.

Add in the chopped toasted almonds, raspberries, blueberries, and the chopped nectarines. Toss gently until well combined.

Serve immediately.

Enjoy!

6. Sautéed Carrot Salad

Eating carrots regularly can lower your blood pressure and cholesterol levels. They are a great ingredient and work well in salads. This one is quick and simple.

5-6 large **carrots**
2 **tomatoes** (sliced)
1 large **yellow onion**
2 tsp **olive oil** or **coconut oil**
1 pinch **salt** to taste (optional)

Makes: 2 servings
Calories: 85 per serving

Wash and cut the carrots into julienne strips. Slice onion into thin rings, then also slice the tomatoes

Heat the oil of your choice in a frying pan. Sauté the carrots, onions and tomatoes over high heat until the onions are tender and browned.

Optionally, add salt to taste before serving.

Enjoy!

7. Tzatziki

Tzatziki is a classic Greek specialty, a sauce with cucumbers, lemon juice, garlic, yoghurt, and dill that can accompany a wide variety of meals. It works very well on warm pita bread and with meat.

1 cup **Greek Yogurt**
½ **garlic** clove (minced)
½ large **cucumber** (peeled, halved lengthwise)
1 tbs fresh **lemon juice**
2 tbs **dill** (chopped)
Salt and **pepper** (ground)

Makes 3 servings
Calories: 135 per serving

Simply combine the ingredients in a bowl. Season with salt and pepper, then add to it to other meals or use it on warm pita bread.

Enjoy!

8. Shell Pasta Salad

Pasta salad with colorful Mediterranean ingredients is as much a meal as it is a treat.

1 lb. (450 g) **shell-shaped pasta**
4 oz. (115 g) **feta** (crumbled)
10 fresh **basil leaves**
1 cup sun-dried, oil-packed **tomatoes** (chopped)
½ cup **black** or **green olives**, (pitted, chopped)
½ cup **extra virgin olive oil**
¼ cup **red wine vinegar**
2 tbs **lemon juice**
Salt and **pepper**

Makes 8 servings
Calories: 345 per serving

Cook the pasta according to packaging instructions, omitting salt and fat. Cook until it is tender, but not mushy. Drain and transfer to a bowl. Rinse under cold water, then drain again.

Add olives, tomatoes, and feta. Stir in the vinegar, extra virgin olive oil, and lemon juice. Add basil and season with salt and peppers, then toss to mix. Serve cold or at room temperature.

Enjoy!

9. Orzo Pasta Salad

This is another Mediterranean pasta salad, using a rice shaped pasta called Orzo.

1 cup uncooked **orzo**
3 tbs pitted **Kalamata olives** (chopped)
3 tbs **red onion** (chopped)
3 oz. **feta cheese** (crumbled)
6 oz. marinated **artichoke hearts** (chopped)
2 cups bagged **baby spinach** (chopped)
½ cup oil-packed, sun-dried **tomatoes** (chopped)
½ tsp **black pepper** (ground)
¼ tsp **salt**

Makes 12 servings
Calories: 215 per serving

Cook the pasta according to packaging instructions, omitting salt and fat. Cook until it is tender, but not mushy. Drain and transfer to a bowl. Rinse under cold water, then drain again.

Add the olives, spinach, onion, feta cheese, tomatoes, and season with salt and pepper.

Drain and chop artichokes, reserving its marinade. Add both to the bowl.

Serve cold or at room temperature.

Enjoy!

10. Roasted Potatoes

Roasted potatoes make a great snack and can also be used to accompany lunch or dinner. If you want to use big instead of small potatoes for this recipe, cut them into chunks.

3 lbs. (1.35 kg) small **Yukon potatoes** (peeled)
1 ½ tbs **butter** or **coconut butter**
3 tbs **extra virgin olive oil**
¼ cup **lemon juice**
4 tsp **thyme** (chopped)
¾ tsp **salt**
½ tsp **pepper**

Makes 7 servings
Calories: 225 per serving

Preheat the oven to 400F (200°C).

Over medium heat, cook oil and butter in a pan for 4 minutes, or until the butter turns light brown. Stir constantly.

Remove from heat, then add potatoes and toss to coat. Transfer to a jelly-roll pan, spreading the potatoes in a single layer.

Bake for 45 minutes, or until potatoes are tender and turn light brown.

Transfer to a serving bowl. Add thyme, salt, pepper, and lemon juice, then toss to coat. Serve immediately.

Enjoy!

11. Zucchini Tomato Pie

A delicious way to use the zucchini and tomato from your garden.

1 lb. (450 g) **green zucchini** (cut)
1 lb. (450 g) **yellow zucchini** (cut)
1 **tomato** (thinly sliced)
4 **garlic** cloves (minced)
½ cup **dill** (freshly chopped)
2 tsp **olive oil**
¼ cup **flat-leaf parsley** (freshly chopped)
4 **scallions** (thinly sliced)
1 tsp **marjoram** (dried)
1 tsp **coarse salt**
5 large **eggs**
5 large **egg whites** (lightly beaten)
2 oz. (55 g) **feta cheese** (crumbled)
½ tsp each **salt** and **pepper** (ground)

Makes 6 servings
Calories 254 per serving

Preheat oven to 325°F (160°C).

Heat 1 tsp olive oil in a large frying pan over medium heat. Add half the scallions, half the garlic, green zucchini, ½ tsp marjoram, and season with ½ tsp salt and ¼ tsp pepper. Sauté for about 5 minutes, stirring frequently, until zucchini is lightly brown and tender. Transfer the mixture to a large bowl and set aside.

Rinse the pan and repeat the process with the yellow zucchini, using the remaining olive oil, garlic, scallions, marjoram, salt and pepper. Once done, add it to the green zucchini mixture. Allow to cool.

Add eggs, dill, and parsley to the zucchini and mix until blended. Transfer the mixture to a round rimmed baking dish, top with tomato and sprinkle with crumbled feta. Bake the pie for 1 hour, or until it becomes firm. Serve immediately or at room temperature.

Enjoy!

12. Cranberry Canapés with Cheese

This snack combines goat cheese, cranberries, thyme and toasted bread. It is easy to make and has a rich taste.

10 **walnuts**
1/8 tsp **cinnamon** (ground)
8 oz. (230 g) fresh **goat cheese**
4 tsp **olive oil**
20 thin **baguette slices**
½ cup **cranberries** (dried)
1 tsp fresh **thyme** (chopped)
Salt and **pepper**

Makes 8 servings
Calories 215 per serving

Preheat oven to 375°F (190°C).

Place walnut halves on a baking tray and drizzle with 1 tsp oil, then sprinkle with salt, pepper and cinnamon. Bake in the oven for about 5 minutes, or until light brown and fragrant. Remove and allow to cool.

Coat one side of the baguette slices with remaining 3 tsp oil and arrange them on the baking tray. Season with salt and pepper. Bake for about 12 minutes, or until lightly toasted. Remove from the oven and allow to cool for a couple of minutes.

In a bowl, combine cheese, 2 tbs water, and dried cranberries. Sprinkle with thyme, salt and pepper. Mix to blend, then spread on bread slices. Garnish each slice with a walnut halve.

Enjoy!

13. Shrimp Skewers 1

This dish is an outstanding party snack, not only for its taste but its looks. At a pool party, your guests might just feel like they are staying at a Mediterranean hotel.

2 **garlic cloves** (minced)
6 plum **tomatoes** (halved)
3 tbs **olive oil** or **coconut oil**
20 large **shrimps** (peeled, with tails)
2 tbs **lime juice** (1 lime)
1 ½ tbs **ginger** (grated, peeled)
1 tbs **Jalapeño pepper** (minced)
1 tbs **basil** (chopped)
1 tbs **cilantro** (chopped)
Salt and **pepper** (ground)

Makes 10 servings
Calories 216 per serving

Mix ginger and garlic in a bowl. Divide and transfer half of the mixture to a large bowl. Add 2 tbs oil and stir to blend, then add shrimps. Toss to coat.
Cover the shrimps and garlic-ginger mixture and refrigerate both for at least 30 minutes.

Preheat grill to medium and lightly coat the grates with oil.

Place the tomatoes in a bowl, add the remaining oil and season with salt and pepper. Grill tomatoes, cut side up, for about 5 minutes, or until charred and pulp is tender. Remove and allow to cool.

Remove skins and seeds from the tomatoes, discarding both. Chop the skinned tomatoes and add to the reserved garlic-ginger mixture. Stir in the jalapeño, cilantro, basil, and lime juice.

Season shrimps with salt and pepper and thread on skewers, piercing through their tails and tops, one shrimp for each skewer. Grill the shrimp for about 3 minutes on each side, or until opaque.

Serve with a bowl of the relish and enjoy!

14. Shrimp Skewers 2

This shrimp skewer recipe goes equally well on parties as the previous one. It has a Greek style to it, combining spinach, cucumber, feta cheese and Tzatziki.

1 cup **Greek yogurt**
1 cup **cucumber** (diced)
3 tbs **dill** (chopped)
2 tbs **lemon juice**
2 tbs **shallots** (chopped)
1 ¼ tsp **aniseed** (crushed, divided)
4 large **shrimps** (peeled, with tails)
8 cups **baby spinach leaves**
¾ cup **feta cheese** (crumbled)
Olive oil
Salt and **black pepper**

Make 4 servings
Calories: 244 per serving

Preheat grill to medium-high.

For the Tzatziki, combine cucumber, Greek yogurt, 2 tbs lemon juice, dill, ¾ tsp crushed aniseed, and shallots in a small bowl. Season with salt and pepper and refrigerate for 20 minutes. Also see snack recipe #7 (page 75).

Oil the grill. Thread the shrimp on skewers, drizzle with olive oil and season with salt, pepper, and the remaining crushed aniseed.

Grill the shrimp for about 3 minutes on each side, or until opaque. Remove and top each shrimp with 1 tbs Tzatziki. Divide spinach and shrimps among 4 plates and sprinkle with crumbled feta cheese.

Enjoy!

15. Brioche with Herbs

This is a wonderful appetizer served over toasted brioche, tomatoes and assorted herbs.

4 slices **brioche** (1/3 inch / 1 cm)
½ lb. (450 g) **pear tomatoes** (halved)
½ cup **chives**, **thyme**, **basil**, and **dill**
2 tsp **olive oil**
Salt and **pepper** (ground)

Makes 4 servings
Calories 117 per serving

Preheat oven to 375 °F (190 °C).

Place the bread slices on a baking sheet and toast in the oven until golden and crisp. Remove from the oven and allow to cool.

Combine tomatoes, olive oil, and herbs in a small bowl. Season with salt and pepper. Evenly spread a quarter of the mixture onto each brioche slice. Season with additional pepper.

Enjoy!

16. Mediterranean Pizza

A flavorful Mediterranean Pizza that takes only a few minutes to prepare.

¼ tsp **Italian seasoning**
4 oz. (120 g) **goat cheese** (crumbled)
¼ tsp **red pepper** (crushed)
12 inch (30 cm) **pizza crust** (prepared)
3 **plum tomatoes** (sliced)
6 **olives** (pitted, chopped)
14 oz. (400 g) **artichoke hearts** (quartered)
¼ cup **fresh basil**
Cooking spray

Makes 4 servings
Calories: 243 per serving

Preheat oven to 450°F (230°C).

Oil a baking sheet and place the pizza crust on it. Sprinkle the Italian seasoning, crushed red pepper, and crumbled goat cheese over the crust. Leave small borders.

Arrange artichoke hearts, plum tomato slices and chopped olives on the pizza. Bake in the oven for about 10 minutes, or until the borders of the crust have slightly browned and the cheese is melted.

Garnish with chopped basil and serve.

Enjoy!

17. Mediterranean Burgers

These burgers combine ground turkey with feta cheese and fresh spicy cucumber.

1 **cucumber** (diced)
½ cup **feta cheese** (crumbled)
2 tbs **red wine vinegar**
½ cup **parsley** (chopped)
4 tbs **olive oil**
1 ½ lbs. (225 g) **turkey** (ground)
1 cup **hummus** (spicy or roasted red pepper**)**
16 mini **pita pockets** (split open)
2 tsp ground **coriander**
Salt and **pepper** (ground)
1 tsp **dried mint salt**

Makes 16 servings
Calories 203 per serving

In a bowl, combine the feta, cucumber, mint, vinegar, and 1 tbs olive oil. Season with a little salt and pepper, then cover and refrigerate.

In another bowl, combine ½ cup hummus, turkey, parsley, and coriander. Season with a little pepper. Make 16 small patties from the turkey mixture.

In a frying pan, heat the remaining olive oil over medium-high heat. Add the patties and roast them in batches for about 3 minutes each, or until golden-brown and cooked through. Transfer to a plate.

Fill each pita pocket with the remaining hummus, turkey patty, tomato slice, and some of the cucumber mixture.

Enjoy!

18. Quinoa Patties with Greens

This recipe turns ordinary vegan patties into an attractive meal.
You can serve them hot or chilled.

5 oz. (150 g) **baby kale**
2 large **eggs**
1 cup white **quinoa**
2 tsp **vinegar**
2 tsp **thyme** (finely chopped)
5 ½ tbs **olive oil**
1 cup **white beans** (cooked)
3 cloves **garlic** (2 minced, 1 whole)
1 cup **breadcrumbs**
½ cup flat-leaf **parsley** (chopped)
1/3 cup **olives**, (chopped, pitted)
1 cup **red peppers** (chopped, roasted)
2 cups **vegetable broth**
Salt and **pepper** (ground)

Makes 4 servings.
Calories: 274 per serving

Fill the broth into a pot and bring to a boil. Reduce heat to low, stir
in the quinoa and let simmer for about 15 minutes, or until the
quinoa has softened and all the broth is absorbed. Remove from
the heat and transfer the quinoa to a bowl. Allow to cool.

Place the white beans in a large bowl and mash with a fork. Stir in
the minced garlic, eggs, thyme, 1 tsp salt and ½ tsp pepper. Mix to
combine.

Add the parsley, olives, breadcrumbs, and cooled quinoa. Stir to
combine. Shape the mixture into patties and arrange them on the
baking sheet lined with parchment.

Add 2 tbs oil, roasted red peppers, vinegar, the whole garlic clove,
pepper and ¼ tsp salt to a blender. Process until smooth. Transfer
the mixture to a serving cup.

Add 2 tbs oil to a pan and set over medium heat. Once hot, roast half of the patties in the pan for 2-3 minutes on each side, or until golden brown. Repeat for all patties.

Transfer to a plate. Sprinkle the greens with salt and pepper to taste. Drizzle with the remaining 1 ½ tbs oil. Put the patties on the greens and serve with the red pepper sauce on the side.

Enjoy!

19. Olive-Tomato Scones

This recipe combines sun dried tomatoes and olives with flour to make delicious scones that can be served on any occasion.

4 **sun dried tomatoes** (chopped)
4 oz. (110 g) **feta cheese** (cubed)
12 oz. (340 g) **self-raising flour**
1 tbs **baking powder**
1 tbs **olive oil**
10 **olives** (pitted, halved)
11 oz. (300 ml) **milk**
2 oz. (60 g) **butter** or **coconut butter**
1 **egg** (beaten)
¼ tsp **salt**

Makes 8 servings
Calories: 128 per serving

Preheat oven to 430°F (220°C).

Grease a large baking tray with the butter of your choice. In a large bowl, combine all of the ingredients and mix well with a spoon, until a sticky dough is formed.

Dust your hands and working table with flour. Shape the dough into an oval, slice into 8 wedges and arrange them on the baking tray. Make sure they are far apart from each other.

Brush with beaten egg and bake in the oven for about 20 minutes, until well risen and golden brown. Remove from the oven and allow to cool for 10 minutes before serving.

Serve with butter and enjoy!

20. Peaches with Vanilla Yogurt

A simple yoghurt recipe that combines fruits and honey with the taste of vanilla. There is room for much variety: instead of peaches, you can use any kind of berries and other fruits.

2 tbs **honey**
4 **peaches** (halved)
½ tsp **vanilla extract**
1 cup **Greek yogurt**

Makes 6 servings
Calories: 72 per serving

In a small glass bowl, combine the honey, yogurt and vanilla extract and mix well. Top the halved peaches with a spoon of the mixture and serve.

Enjoy!

21. Mediterranean Baguette

This recipe combines French baguette with Mediterranean flavors.

1 **baguette**
½ **clove garlic** (minced)
¼ cup **olives** (chopped, pitted)
2 tbs **olive oil**
1 tbs **lemon juice**
2 tbs **parsley** (chopped)
1 cup **red pepper** (chopped, roasted)
1 tbs **capers** (rinsed, drained)
1 ½ cup **white beans** (rinsed, drained)
¼ tsp **pepper** (freshly ground)
1 tsp **lemon zest**
Salt

Makes 12 servings
Calories: 127 per serving

Preheat oven to 400°F (200°C)

Slice the baguette diagonally into about 24 thin slices. Coat the slices with olive oil and sprinkle with minced garlic and salt. Bake in the oven for about 5 minutes, or until lightly golden brown.

In a bowl, combine the olives, beans, capers, pepper, lemon zest, 2 tbs olive oil, lemon juice, and parsley. Season with pepper and mix well.

Spoon the mixture over the toasted baguette slices.

Enjoy!

22. Fish Wraps

This seafood snack has much variety, as you can use all kinds of fish for it.

2 tbs **Greek yogurt**
4 **whole grain wraps**
8 tsp **olive tapenade**
2 cup **baby arugula**
1 tbs **fresh basil** (chopped)
1 tsp **lemon juice**
¼ tsp **lemon zest**
6 oz. (170 g) any **fish** (shredded)
½ cup **white beans**
½ cup **celery** (chopped)
2 tbs **red onion** (chopped)

Makes 4 servings
Calories: 164 per serving

In a medium bowl, combine the lemon juice, lemon zest and yogurt. Whisk in the beans, onion, shredded fish meat, baby arugula, basil and celery.

Place the wraps on a plate and spread ½ tbs of the tapenade over each wrap. Add some of the arugula and fish mixture and roll the wrap into the shape of a tube. Repeat for each wrap.

Enjoy!

Side Dishes

1. Cucumber-Feta Salad

This is a refreshing salad for any occasion.

½ cup **feta** (crumbled)
1 ½ lb. (680 g) **cucumbers** (quartered, seeded)
1 tsp fresh **oregano** (chopped)
½ cup **red onion** (thinly sliced)
2 tbs **dill** (chopped)
2 tbs **red wine vinegar**
2 tbs **mint** (chopped)
3 tbs **olive oil**
Salt and **black pepper** to taste

Makes 6 servings
Calories: 131 per serving

Cut each cucumber lengthwise into 4 pieces, then chop crosswise into thin slices and place in a large bowl.

Add the oregano, onion, feta, dill, mint, and vinegar. Season with salt and pepper to taste. Drizzle with olive oil and toss to coat.

Enjoy!

2. Mediterranean Grain Salad

This salad contains farro, a Mediterranean grain that is naturally rich in fiber and contains more protein than wheat.

½ cup + 1 tbs **olive oil**
1/3 cup **red wine vinegar**
1 cup **radicchio** (shredded)
3 cups **farro** (semi-pearled)
1 cup **cannellini beans** (cooked)
1 tsp **lemon zest** (grated)
½ cup **olives** (chopped)
1 cup **artichoke hearts**
1 cup **fennel** (diced)
¾ cup **pine nuts** (toasted)
¼ cup fresh **basil** (chopped)
Salt and **pepper**

Makes 9 servings
Calories: 324 per serving

Wash the farro under cold water and drain in a colander.

Bring water to a boil in a large pot over high heat. Stir in ¾ tsp salt. Add the farro, reduce heat and let simmer for 30 minutes, or until softened. If needed, add more water so the mixture does not dry out or stick to the bottom.

Transfer the farro to a large serving bowl, drizzle with 1 tbs olive oil and allow to cool.

In a small bowl, combine ½ cup olive oil, vinegar, olives, lemon zest, and season with salt and pepper.

Crumble the farro with a fork to break up any lumps. Mix in the fennel, cannellini, artichokes, basil, radicchio, and pine nuts.

Pour ½ cup of the prepared vinaigrette over the salad and toss to combine. Adjust seasonings to taste. Serve immediately or refrigerate for up to 1 day.

Enjoy!

3. Flavorful Potato Dish

These red potatoes are loaded with spices.

2 lbs. (900 g) **red potatoes** (peeled, sliced)
20 **olives** (pitted)
1 small **onion** (grated)
1 medium **onion** (sliced)
3 tbs **olive oil**
1/3 cup **tomatoes** (grated)
1 pinch **cumin** (ground)
1 tsp **garlic** (crushed)
3 **bay leaves**
¼ tsp **ginger** (ground)
¼ sp **paprika**
½ **lemon**
2 tbs **flat leaf parsley** (chopped)
¼ tsp **saffron threads**
2 tbs **cilantro** (chopped)
½ tsp **salt**

Makes 6 servings
Calories: 176 per serving

Peel the potatoes, cut in thick slices, transfer to a bowl of cold water and set aside.

Heat the olive oil in a pot over medium heat. Stir in the grated onions and sauté for about 4 minutes, or until translucent. Add the garlic, ginger, tomato, paprika, cumin and cook for another 2 minutes, stirring frequently.

Remove the potatoes from the cold water, drain and add to the tomato mixture. Stir in the sliced onions, ½ lemon, and bay leaves.

Sprinkle the mixture with the cilantro and parsley, then season with salt to taste. Add 1 ½ cups hot water and the saffron. Stir and reduce the heat to low. Simmer for about 40 minutes, or until the potatoes have softened.

Transfer the potatoes to a serving dish and cover to keep warm. Discard the lemon.

Add the olives to the sauce in the pot and cook until it thickens. Adjust the seasoning to taste, then spoon the sauce over the potatoes.

Enjoy!

4. Couscous-Tomato Salad

A simple but tasty couscous salad with tomatoes, artichoke hearts, Kalamata olives, basil, and a light lemon dressing.

1 lb. (450 g) **couscous**
2 cups **grape tomatoes** (halved)
2 cups **artichoke hearts** (chopped)
1 ½ cups **olives** (chopped, pitted)
½ cup fresh **basil** (chopped)

Dressing
3 cloves **garlic** (minced)
½ cup **olive oil**
2 tsp **oregano** (chopped)
1 tbs **basil** (chopped)
Juice of 2 **lemons**
Salt and **Pepper** (to taste)

Makes 12 servings
Calories: 262 per serving

Prepare couscous according to package directions.

Transfer couscous to a large bowl, then add olives, artichoke hearts, basil and tomatoes.

In a small bowl, combine the ingredients for the dressing and stir to blend.

Pour the dressing over the couscous mixture and mix well to combine. Season the salad with salt and pepper to taste and serve.

Enjoy!

5. Red Potato and Olive Salad

This refreshing dish is great for picnics and garden gatherings. It can be served warm or chilled.

2 lbs. (900 g) round **red potatoes**
1/3 cup **olive oil**
1 ½ cups **olives** (chopped, pitted)
2 tbs **flat-leaf parsley** (chopped)
3 tbs **white wine vinegar**
1/3 cup **red onion** (chopped)
Salt and **Pepper** (ground)

Makes: 6 servings
Calories: 243 per serving

Place the potatoes in a large pot of water, stir in 1 tbs of salt, cover and bring to a boil.

Uncover, reduce heat and simmer for about 15 minutes, or until the potatoes are tender. Remove the water and allow the potatoes to cool slightly. Cut the potatoes into thin slices and transfer to a large bowl.

For the dressing, combine the vinegar, onion, olive oil, and olives in a small bowl. Season with salt and pepper to taste.

Pour the olive dressing over the potatoes, sprinkle with parsley and mix to combine. Serve the salad warm or chilled.

Enjoy!

6. Oven Carrots

This side dish offers a great blend of flavors and goes well with fish or poultry.

1 ½ lbs. (680 g) **carrots** (peeled, halved)
¼ tsp **nutmeg** (ground)
1 pinch of **cayenne** (ground)
¼ cup **olive oil**
1/4 tsp. **cinnamon** (ground)
½ cup **chicken** or **vegetable broth**
3 medium cloves **garlic** (sliced)
Salt (to taste)

Makes: 4 servings
Calories: 176 per serving

Preheat oven to 375°F (190°C), setting a rack at the center.

Arrange the carrots in a single layer in a baking dish and place the garlic slices among the carrots.

In a small bowl, combine the olive oil and broth, then sprinkle with cayenne, cinnamon, nutmeg, and ½ tsp salt. Stir to combine and pour over the carrots.

Cover the baking dish with foil and bake for about 45 minutes in the oven, or until the carrots are soft.

Remove the foil and continue baking for another 15 minutes, or until the carrots become golden. Remove from the oven, allow to cool for 5 minutes, then transfer to a serving dish.

Enjoy!

7. Grilled Eggplant and Zucchini

A great refreshing summer side dish that is quick and easy to prepare. It is great to serve it with pasta or rice.

1 clove **garlic** (minced)
¼ cup **olive oil**
1 large **eggplant**
¼ tsp **red pepper flakes**
3 medium **zucchinis**
1 cup **parsley** (finely chopped)
3 tbs **balsamic vinegar**
1/4 tsp **salt**
1 tsp **sea salt**
¼ tsp **pepper**

Makes: 6 servings
Calories: 142 per serving

Slice the peeled eggplant into thin rounds. Sprinkle with salt on both sides and arrange on a flat platter. Cover with kitchen towel and let sit for about 30 minutes.

Cut the zucchinis lengthwise into three slices. Rinse under cold water and drain.

Coat the grill pan with oil and set over medium-high heat. Grill the zucchinis for about 5 minutes and the eggplant for about 7 minutes per side, or until golden-brown.

In a small cup, combine the vinegar, olive oil, garlic, red pepper flakes, parsley, salt and pepper.

Dip the ends of each grilled vegetable into the dressing and place on a serving plate. Spoon the remaining dressing over the vegetables and serve.

Enjoy!

8. Stuffed Tomatoes

These stuffed tomatoes are delicious whether you serve them hot or chilled. You can serve this dish with a potato salad and greens.

1 **bay leaf**
1 tsp **olive oil**
1 cup **white rice**
1 ½ cups **chicken stock**
1 ¼ cup **white wine**
½ cup **Parmesan cheese** (grated)
6 medium **tomatoes**
¼ cup **green onions** (chopped)
¼ cup **basil leaves** (chopped)

Makes: 6 servings
Calories: 215 per serving

Cut a slice off the tops of the tomatoes and seed them with a teaspoon. Thinly chop the pulp and place in a pot. Place the hollowed tomatoes on a baking dish, cut side down.

Place the rice in a pot and cook for 1 minute over medium high-heat. Add the stock, olive oil, the bay leaf, and ¼ cup of the wine. Bring to a boil, then reduce the heat, cover and let it simmer for about 30 minutes, or until all the liquid is absorbed.

Discard the bay leaf. Remove from heat and let the rice cool for at least 10 minutes.

Preheat the oven to 350°F (180°C).
Add the green onions, 1/3 cup of the Parmesan and basil to the cooled rice, stir well to combine.

Fill the tomatoes with the cooked rice mixture. Sprinkle each tomato with 1 tsp of Parmesan cheese. Place the filled tomatoes on a baking dish and return the cut tops on each tomato.

Lightly cover the dish with aluminum foil. Bake the tomatoes in the oven for about 20 minutes. Remove the foil, drizzle the tomatoes with the remaining wine, and continue baking for another 10 minutes. Let the dish cool for 5 minutes.

9. Eggplant and Olives

A tasty side-dish that is great when served with chicken, rice or noodles.

1 medium **eggplant** (sliced)
¼ tsp **red-pepper flakes**
2 small **shallots** (sliced crosswise)
6 **Olives** (pitted, chopped)
1 **garlic** clove (minced)
3 tbs **red wine vinegar**
1 tbs **capers** (rinsed)
¼ cup + 4 tsp **olive oil**
2 tbs golden **raisins**
Salt

Makes: 4 servings
Calories: 221 per serving

Slice the eggplant into 8 pieces. Place them in a colander, season with salt, mix to coat and set over a bowl. Let stand for 30 minutes, then rinse in cold water and drain.

Combine the garlic, vinegar, 3 tbs water, shallots, and red-pepper flakes to a medium pan and bring to a boil. Cook the mixture for 1 minute, then turn off the heat. Add the capers, raisins, olives and ¼ cup olive oil. Stir and allow to cool.

Heat grill on high and oil the grates. Coat the eggplant with the remaining 4 tsp olive oil. Grill eggplant slices for about 10 minutes, turning once, until soft and brown.

Transfer the eggplant on a serving platter, sprinkle with prepared shallot mixture. Allow to cool to room temperature and serve all together.

Enjoy!

10. Stuffed Peppers

These roasted Mediterranean peppers are stuffed with beef, couscous, chickpeas and seasonings. They are great to be served with a green salad.

8 oz. (250 g) **beef** (ground)
15 oz. (430 g) **chickpeas**
18 oz. (510 g) **tomato sauce**
2 tsp **cumin**
2 tsp **olive oil**
1/3 cup **couscous**
1 ½ tsp **cinnamon**
1 medium **onion** (chopped)
2 cloves **garlic** (minced)
2 tsp **ginger** (grated)
8 dried **apricots** (grated)
4 green **bell peppers**
Cooking spray

Makes 4 servings
Calories: 317 per serving

Add couscous to a pot of lightly salted boiling water. Remove from heat, cover, and let stand about 5 minutes, until water has been absorbed.

In a small bowl, mix together salt, cumin and cinnamon.

Heat olive oil in a large saucepan over medium-high heat. Stir in the garlic and fry for 1 minute, or until golden.

Stir in the ground beef and cook for about 4 minutes, breaking it up with spoon along the way. Once the meat becomes pale, add the ginger and onion, then cook for another 4 minutes, or until the onion is tender. Pour the cumin mixture over the beef and cook for 1 more minute.

Add ½ cup water, apricots, tomato sauce and chickpeas. Stir well to combine and remove the pan from heat. Add the couscous to the beef and mix well.

Preheat oven to 375°F (180 °C).

Lightly coat a baking dish with cooking spray. Fill the bell peppers with beef mixture and arrange them on the dish. Add ¼ cup water to the dish, cover with aluminum foil and bake in the oven for about 40 minutes, or until peppers are soft and cooked.

Enjoy!

11. Orzo Pasta Salad

This is a wonderful pasta salad full of summer flavors.

½ cup **dill** (chopped)
2 cups **cherry tomatoes** (halved)
3 tbs **extra-virgin olive oil**
1 ½ cups **feta cheese** (crumbled)
1 tsp **lemon zest** (grated)
1 cup **orzo pasta**
½ tsp each **salt** and **pepper**

Makes 5 servings
Calories: 246 per serving

Cook the orzo according to package instructions until al dente.

Meanwhile, in a large salad bowl, combine tomatoes, oil, dill, grated lemon zest, and season with ½ tsp each of salt and pepper. Let the mixture stand for 15 minutes.

Drain the cooked orzo in the colander and add it to the bowl with the tomato mixture. Sprinkle the salad with feta, mix well to coat and serve.

Enjoy!

12. Rice and Saffron

This side dish is perfect to be served with meat or fish.

10 **saffron threads** (crushed)
1 lb. (450 g) **long-grain rice**
5 cups **vegetable stock**
3 oz. (80 g) **butter** or **coconut butter**
Parsley (finely chopped, to garnish)
Parmesan cheese (grated, to garnish)
Salt and **pepper**

Makes 6 servings
Calories: 215 per serving

Melt the butter in a large pot over high heat. Add the rice and stir-fry for about 3 minutes, or until it becomes opaque. Add 4 cups of the stock, season with a pinch of salt and bring to a boil.

Reduce the heat, cover and let simmer for about 20 minutes, or until all the liquid is absorbed. Add the saffron to the remaining 1 cup of stock and pour over the rice. Give a stir, place a kitchen towel over the pot, cover, and turn off the heat.

Let it stand for 10 minutes before serving. Place in a serving bowl, sprinkle with grated Parmesan, garnish with chopped parsley and serve.

Enjoy!

Dinner Recipes

1. Mediterranean Nachos

Nachos are a simple yet flavorful dish. It is very easy to prepare and extremely satisfying. Though traditionally a Mexican dish, followers of the Mediterranean diet can still enjoy nachos by using this recipe.

Fresh **parsley leaves** (optional, chopped)
2 tbs **red onions** (minced)
¼ cup **tomatoes** (diced)
8 pitted **Kalamata olives** (sliced in half)
2 tbs **feta cheese** (grated)
2 tbs **hummus**
1 taco-sized **tortilla** ·
Extra virgin **olive oil** (for greasing)

Makes: 2 servings
Calories: 155 per serving

Slice the flour tortilla into 8 equal wedge-shaped pieces.

Preheat the oven to 400 F (200 °C). Grease a baking tray lightly with extra virgin olive oil.

Arrange the tortilla wedges onto the baking tray and brush the tops very lightly with more extra virgin olive oil.

Bake the tortilla wedges for 5 minutes, or until they are golden brown and slightly toasted.

Spread roughly half a tsp of hummus onto each nacho, then top with half a tsp of grated feta cheese. Top all nachos equally with the minced red onions, diced tomatoes, and halved olives. Bake for another 5 minutes.

Sprinkle chopped fresh parsley leaves on top.

Serve immediately and enjoy!

2. Barley and Eggplant Salad

This is a hearty dish with strong flavors. For vegetarians, the chicken broth can be replaced by water.

¼ tsp **cayenne pepper**
½ lb. (225 g) **pearl barley**
14 oz. (400 g) low-sodium **chicken broth**
¾ cup **water**
2 tbs **lemon juice** (freshly squeezed)
1 clove of **garlic** (minced)
1 cup fresh **parsley leaves** (chopped)
½ cup fresh **mint leaves** (chopped)
½ lb. (225 g) **cherry tomatoes** (quartered)
1/3 cup **olives** (sliced in half)
½ cup **red onions** (sliced)
½ tsp **coriander** (ground)
1 ½ tsp **cumin seeds**
1 cup **scallions** (chopped)
1 tsp **black pepper** (ground)
1 tsp **table salt**
10 tbs extra virgin **olive oil**
¾ lb. (340 g) **zucchini** (diced)
1 ½ lbs. (680 g) **eggplant** (diced)

Makes: 12 servings
Calories: 215 per serving

Preheat the oven to 425F (220°C). Place the oven racks in the lower and upper thirds of the oven.

In a large mixing bowl, combine the diced zucchini and eggplant and add in ¾ tsp ground black pepper, ¾ tsp table salt, and 5 tbs extra virgin olive oil. Mix well.

Divide the mixture into two greased baking trays. Roast the vegetable mixture in the preheated oven, with occasional stirring and switching the position of the baking trays halfway through the baking time, for about 25 minutes, or until the vegetables are tender and golden brown. Transfer all vegetables to just one baking tray, and reserve the other tray for later.

Heat 2 tbs of olive oil in a large pot, then add the cayenne pepper, ground coriander, cumin seeds, and chopped scallions. Stir well and cook for 1 minute. Add the pearl barley and cook for 2 more minutes with constant stirring.

Add the water and chicken broth and allow to boil. Once boiling, reduce to low heat and simmer for about 35 minutes, or until the barley is soft and all of the liquids have been absorbed.

Turn off the heat, cover and let it sit for 5 minutes. Transfer the cooked barley to the reserved baking tray and spread evenly to cover the bottom. Allow it to cool for about 20 minutes, or until it has reached room temperature.

To prepare the dressing, in a large mixing bowl, combine the remaining 3 tbs extra virgin olive oil, ¼ tsp ground black pepper, ¼ tsp table salt, minced garlic, and freshly squeezed lemon juice. Mix well until fully combined.

Add in the roasted vegetables, cooked barley, and the remaining ingredients to the dressing and toss well until fully combined. Serve immediately with slices of your choice of cheese.

Serve immediately.

Enjoy!

3. Cherry Tomato, Garlic, and Eggplant Salad

This simple yet flavorful salad goes well with steak, lamb, or any Mediterranean meat main dish, but can be eaten and enjoyed on its own.

2 tbs **red wine vinegar**
2 tbs **dill** (chopped)
2 tbs **parsley leaves** (chopped)
¼ cup **onions** (chopped)
1 pint (530 g) **cherry tomatoes** (sliced in half)
6 cloves of **garlic** (peeled)
2 tbs **extra virgin olive oil**
1 ¼ lbs. (570 g) **eggplants** (peeled, sliced)

Makes: 4 servings
Calories: 135 per serving

Preheat the oven to 350F (180°C). Arrange eggplant pieces in a roasting pan. Drizzle the extra virgin olive oil on top and toss lightly to coat the eggplant pieces. Roast in the preheated oven for 20 minutes.

Add in the peeled garlic cloves and continue roasting for an additional 25 minutes, or until the garlic and eggplant are soft. Once done roasting, allow it to cool for 10 minutes.

Chop the roasted garlic cloves finely, then transfer roasted eggplants and garlic to a large bowl.

Add the remaining ingredients into the eggplant and garlic mixture and stir well until fully combined. Add ground black pepper and table salt to taste. Allow it to cool to room temperature before serving.

Enjoy!

4. Roasted Tomatoes and Broccoli

This recipe combines tomatoes, broccoli and olives into a delicious Mediterranean dish.

1 tsp dried **oregano**
¼ tsp **table salt**
10 pitted **black olives** (sliced in half)
1 tbs **lemon juice** (freshly squeezed)
½ tsp **lemon rind**
2 **garlic cloves** (minced)
1 tbs **extra virgin olive oil**
1 cup **grape tomatoes**
4 cups **broccoli crowns** (chopped)

Makes: 4 servings
Calories: 80 per serving

Preheat the oven to 450F (230°C). In a large mixing bowl, combine the table salt, minced garlic, extra virgin olive oil, grape tomatoes, and chopped broccoli. Stir well to combine.

Spread evenly across a baking pan and bake for about 12 minutes, or until the broccoli just starts to brown.

While baking, mix together the dried oregano, halved olives, squeezed lemon juice, and grated lemon rind in a large mixing bowl. Add the baked vegetables and stir well until fully combined. Let it cool for a 5 minutes before serving.

Enjoy!

5. Mediterranean Wrap

This recipe is a filling and delicious meal that takes only 5 minutes to make. These wraps are perfect for the Mediterranean diet and should get a spot in any meal plan.

1 tbs **vinaigrette**
1 ¼ tbs **basil leaves** (chopped)
2 tbs pitted **black olives** (sliced in half)
¼ cup **tomatoes** (chopped)
1/3 cup **feta cheese** (crumbled)
½ **avocado** (sliced, diced)
¾ cup fresh **baby spinach** (chopped)
1 9-inch (23 cm) **spinach wrap** or **tortilla wrap**
1 tbs regular **cream cheese**

Makes: 1 serving
Calories: 365 per serving

Spread the cream cheese evenly on one side of the spinach or tortilla wrap. Add the cubed avocado, crumbled feta cheese, chopped basil leaves, chopped spinach, vinaigrette, and halved olives.

Roll up the wrap carefully and slice in half diagonally.

Serve immediately and enjoy!

6. Paleo Slow Cooker Chicken

Mediterranean recipes are often dominated by ingredients such as lemon, olives and tomatoes. Serve this dish with mashed sweet potatoes.

1 **lemon**
¼ cup **olives**
15 oz. (425 g) **plum tomatoes** (roughly chopped)
¼ tsp **black pepper** (ground)
¾ cup **onion** (chopped)
2 tbs **drained capers**
12 bone in **chicken thighs**
1 tbs **olive oil** or **coconut oil**
Rosemary (optional, chopped)
Fresh parsley (optional, chopped)

Makes 6 servings
Calories: 215 per serving

Grate the lemon to get 1 tbs of zest. Also, squeeze the lemon to get 1 tbs of juice. Combine the zest and juice in a bowl. Cover and refrigerate.

Combine the onion, lemon juice, olives, drained capers and plum tomatoes in a slow cooker. Season the chicken thighs with pepper.

Heat the oil of your choice in a pan over medium heat. Place the chicken thighs in a pan, then cook for 3 minutes on each side until brown.

Add the chicken thighs to the slow cooker. Cook for 4 hours on medium heat until brown and tender.

Place the chicken on plates and stir in the lemon sauce. Garnish with desired amount of rosemary and parsley.

Enjoy!

7. Italian Tomato Meatballs

Most meatballs combine pork, beef and veal. This recipe uses a lighter sauce to intensify the flavor without adding much on calories and fat.

1 **egg**
1 tsp **salt**
1 **small onion** (minced)
6 **garlic cloves** (minced)
1 lb. (450 g) **lean ground beef**
½ tbs **olive oil** or **coconut oil**
14 oz. (400 g) **dice tomatoes**
2 tsp **Italian seasoning**
1 **bay leaf**
1 **egg white**
¼ **parsley** (minced)
2 lb. (900 g) **chicken** or **turkey sausage**
28 oz. (800g) **tomatoes** (crushed)
1 tsp **red pepper flakes**
1 cup **chicken broth**

Makes 8 servings
Calories: 210 per serving

Whisk the egg and egg white together in a bowl. Add the parsley, garlic cloves and ¼ of the onion.

Combine the beef and sausage. Stir to mix. Roll the mixture into meatballs. It should be enough for 22-25 of them, depending on the size. Transfer to a slow cooker.

Heat the oil of your choice in a pan over medium heat. Sauté the remaining ¾ of the onion for 5 minutes until fragrant and tender.

Add the red pepper flakes, Italian seasoning, and garlic. Stir for 30 seconds before adding the diced tomatoes, bay leaf, crushed tomatoes and chicken broth.

Pour the sauce over the meatballs in the slow cooker and cook for 6 hours in low heat.

8. Carrot Garlic Soup

This is a delicious and healthy meal for the whole family.

2 lbs. (910 g) **carrots**
3 **garlic cloves** (finely chopped)
1 tsp **curry powder**
½ cup **sour cream** or **coconut cream**
8 oz. (225 g) **shrimps** (peeled, cooked)
6 **white and green scallions**
2 tbs **fresh ginger** (chopped)
2 ½ cups low sodium **chicken broth**
1 pinch **salt**
Cilantro to sprinkle (optional)

Makes 6 servings
Calories: 177 per serving

Combine the scallions, ginger, curry powder, garlic and carrots in a slow cooker.
Add 2 cups of water, then bring to a boil. Cook for 7 to 8 hours in low heat until carrots are tender.

Remove from heat and allow it to cool slightly.

Puree the soup in batches, then return to the slow cooker. Add the sour cream or coconut cream and season with salt until completely heated through.

Ladle the soup into bowls and top with optional cilantro.

Enjoy!

9. Slow Cooker Zucchini Dish

This dish combines many flavors, ranging from the exotic quality of coconuts to the tanginess of herbs.

2 zucchinis
5 cups (1.2 liters) **chicken broth**
½ cup **shallots** (chopped)
1 tsp **oregano** (crushed, dried)
3 tbs **butter** or **coconut butter**
1 tbs **extra virgin olive oil**
1 **yellow sweet pepper** (chopped)
2 cups **rice**
3 **garlic cloves** (minced)
3 cups **mushrooms** (sliced)
Italian flat leaf parsley

Makes 12 servings
Calories: 215 per serving

Lightly coat a slow cooker with olive oil or cooking spray.

Add the zucchini, rice, oregano, salt and pepper, chicken broth, garlic, and shallots. Cover and cook for 4 hours in high heat.

Add the butter, then remove from heat. Set aside for 15 minutes. Pour in the vegetable broth, if the dish is too dry.

Heat the oil of your choice in a pan. Cook the sliced mushrooms, then transfer to plate. Top with sweet pepper and parsley.

Enjoy!

10. Lamb Chops in Greek Sauce

This recipes gives lamb a Greek touch, using a minty sauce. Alternatively, you can use Tzatziki from *snack recipe #7* for this.

8 4 oz. (115 g) **lamb loin chops** (trimmed)
½ cup **Greek yogurt**
2 tsp **oregano** (chopped)
3 **garlic** cloves (minced)
2 tsp **extra virgin olive oil**
1 tbs **mint** (chopped)
2 ½ tbs **lemon juice**
¼ tsp **sea salt**
¼ tsp **black pepper** (ground)

Makes 4 servings
Calories: 325 per serving

Combine 2 tbs lemon juice, oregano, and garlic in a bowl.

Season lamb chops with salt and pepper, then coat with the mixture from the bowl.

Heat the olive oil in a pan over high heat. Add lamb chops and cook for 3-4 minutes on each side, or until desired level of doneness.

Remove from heat and allow to cool for 5 minutes.

Force the serve, combine yogurt, mint, and the remaining ½ tbs lemon juice in a bowl. Alternatively, use Tzatziki. Serve sauce with the lamb.

Enjoy!

11. Ginger Chicken with Olives

This dish has a great blend of flavors that is not only delicious but also makes your house smell good.

½ cup **green olives** (pitted, chopped)
1 tbs **olive oil**
4 whole **chicken legs**
1 **yellow onion** (cut)
3 **carrots** (diced)
2 **garlic cloves** (minced)
½ inch (1.2 cm) **ginger** (chopped)
1 cup **chicken broth**
1 cup **dry white wine**
4 sprigs **thyme**
1/3 cup **raisins**
¾ cup **chickpeas**

Makes 4 servings
Calories: 224per serving

Preheat oven to 350°F (180°C).

Heat olive oil in an oven proof pan over medium heat. Add the chicken legs, leaving some space between the pieces of the chicken and sauté for 5 minutes, or until they get golden crust on both sides. Remove and allow to cool.

Reduce the heat to medium and add ginger, carrots, onion, and garlic to the pan. Stir-fry for about 5 minutes, or until the vegetables get soft. Add 1 cup water, chicken broth, and wine. Bring the mixture to a boil.

Transfer the chicken back to the pan, seasoning with thyme. Once the mixture begins to bubble, cover and transfer to the oven. Bake for 40-45 minutes. Uncover, add the chickpeas, raisins, and olives. Return the uncovered pan back to the oven bake for another 20 minutes.

Remove the thyme and serve.

Enjoy!

12. Citrus Patties

After serving this on a party, it become one of my most requested recipes among my family and friends.

1 egg **yolk**
1 small **carrot** (shredded)
3 tbs **olive oil**
1/3 cup **almonds** (toasted, sliced)
1 small **onion** (chopped)
1 medium **stalk celery**, (chopped)
2/3 cup **couscous**
2 **cloves garlic** (chopped)
1 cup soft **bread crumbs**
1 tbs **fresh chives** (chopped)
1 **egg**
½ tsp **salt**
¼ tsp **pepper**

Sauce:
1/8 tsp **salt**
2 tbs **currants**
2 tsp **cornstarch**
1 1/2 tsp **chives** (chopped)
1 tbs **lemon juice**
¾ cup **orange juice**
1 tsp **orange zest** (grated)

Makes 4 servings
Calories: 295 per serving

Slightly coat a baking sheet with olive oil.

Fill water into a pot and bring to a boil. Add the couscous, salt, and pepper. Remove from heat, cover and allow to cool for at least 5 minutes.

Heat olive oil in a saucepan over medium heat. Stir in the onion, garlic, celery, and carrot. Sauté while stirring, until vegetables have softened.

In a large bowl, combine vegetables, couscous, almonds, egg, egg yolk, bread crumbs, and chives. Mix well. Scoop the couscous mixture into your hands and form 8 patties. Arrange on the baking sheet, cover and chill them for 2 hours.

Meanwhile, prepare the sauce. In a small bowl, combine salt, lemon and orange juices, orange zest, cornstarch, chives and currants.

Remove the patties from the fridge. Heat oil in a large frying pan over medium heat. Place patties in the pan and fry for about 8 minutes, turning once, until golden brown on both sides.

Serve with the sauce and enjoy!

13. Salmon with Zucchini and Olives

A healthy and fulfilling salmon dinner with good Mediterranean ingredients.

4 **salmon fillets** (6 oz. / 170 g)
2 cups **cherry tomatoes** (halved)
1/2 cup **zucchini** (finely chopped)
2 tbs **capers**
1 tbs **olive oil**
3 oz. (85 g) sliced **olives** (drained)
¼ tsp each **salt** and **pepper**

Makes 4 servings
Calories: 289 per serving

Preheat the oven to 425°F (220°C).

Season the fish fillets with salt and pepper on both sides. Oil a baking and arrange the fillets on it.

In a bowl, combine cherry tomatoes, zucchini, capers, and olive oil. Stir and pour the mixture over the fish.

Bake in the oven for about 20 minutes, or until cooked through.

Enjoy!

14. Seafood and Potatoes

This is a fabulous Greek dish for lunch, dinner, and parties.

1 lb. (450 g) **gold potatoes**
8 **garlic cloves** (peeled)
¼ cup **plain Greek yogurt**
3 tbs **olive oil** (divided)
¼ tsp **thyme** (dried)
1 lb. (450 g) **halibut fillets** (quartered)
1 lb. (450 g) small **zucchini** (cut)
Zest of 1 **lemon**
Juice of 1 **lemon**
1 slice **sourdough bread** (crust removed)
2 red **bell peppers** (quartered)
1 tsp **salt** (divided)
½ red **onion** (sliced)

Makes 4 servings
Calories: 327 per serving

Preheat grill to medium-high heat.

Cut the peeled potatoes in 1-inch (2.5 cm) pieces and place in a large pot. Pour enough cold water to cover the pieces. Add the garlic and cook over high heat for about 15 minutes, or until potatoes are tender.

Cut bread into small pieces and place in a bowl. Transfer 3 tbs liquid from the potato mixture over the bread and crumble with a fork until smooth. Stir in lemon zest and juice, yogurt, and 2 tbs olive oil. Mix to blend.

Transfer the cooked potatoes and garlic to a colander and drain, reserving the liquid.
Add potatoes to bread mixture and mash, adding 2 tbs of reserved liquid until you get soft puree. Sprinkle with 2 tsp olive oil and ½ tsp salt. Stir and cover to keep warm.

Season fish with remaining ½ tsp salt and thyme and coat with ½ tsp olive oil. Grill the fish for about 3 minutes on each side. Remove from the pan and cover to keep warm.

In a large bowl, combine zucchini, bell pepper, and red onion. Sprinkle with the remaining olive oil and mix to coat.

Place the bell peppers in grill pan over medium heat and cook for about 5 minutes. Add the onion and zucchini, then grill for another 10 minutes, or until vegetables have softened.

Serve all together and enjoy!

15. Sardine and Pasta

A hearty spicy meal made with pasta and sardines.

8 oz. (230 g) **fettuccine pasta**
8 oz. (225 g) boneless **sardines** (flaked)
¼ cup **Parmesan cheese** (shredded)
4 tbs **olive oil** or **coconut oil**
4 cloves **garlic** (minced)
½ cup fresh **parsley** (chopped)
1 cup fresh **breadcrumbs**
¼ cup **lemon juice**
½ tsp **salt**
1 tsp **pepper**

Makes: 4 servings
Calories: 375 per serving

Place the pasta in a large pot of boiling water and cook according to package directions. Drain in a colander.

While cooking the pasta, heat 2 tbs oil in a frying pan over medium heat. Add garlic and stir-fry for about 30 seconds, or until lightly brown and fragrant.

Heat the remaining 2 tbs oil in the pan over medium heat. Stir in the breadcrumbs and fry for about 5 minutes, or until golden and crispy. Remove from the pan.

In a small bowl, combine the salt, pepper, lemon juice, and fried garlic oil. Add the pasta, sardines, parsley, and Parmesan. Stir to combine.

Serve and sprinkle each dish with breadcrumbs.

Enjoy!

16. Mediterranean Kebabs

These kebabs are fun to make and perfect for garden barbeque parties.

¼ cup **lemon juice**
2 tbs **oregano** (chopped)
2 tbs **olive oil**
1 ½ lbs. (680 g) skinless **chicken breast** (cut)
21 slices **zucchini** (½ inch / 1 cm thick)
1 **fennel bulb** (cut)
14 **garlic cloves** (peeled)
½ tsp **salt**
¼ tsp **black pepper**
Cooking spray

Makes 7 servings
Calories: 174 per serving

Cut the chicken breast into 28 strips. In a bowl, combine the chicken strips, oregano, olive oil, zucchini, and fennel. Toss to coat. Refrigerate for 30 minutes to absorb flavors.

Heat a grill to medium-high and coat with oil.

Place garlic cloves in pot of boiling water and cook for 3 minutes. Drain and allow to cool.

Thread 3 zucchini slices, 2 fennel wedges, 4 chicken strips, and 2 garlic cloves alternately onto 7 skewers and season with salt and pepper. Place kebabs on grill rack and grill for about 8 minutes, or your desired level of doneness.

Enjoy!

17. Chickpea Pasta with Tomatoes

This hearty and flavorful pasta dish is prepared in about 20 minutes.

3 cups **pasta** (cooked)
2 tbs **balsamic vinegar**
2 **garlic cloves** (minced)
½ cup **basil** (chopped)
2 tsp **olive oil**
1 lb. (450 g) **chickpeas** (drained)
2 oz. (60 g) **Asiago cheese** (grated)
2 cups **tomato** (chopped)
½ tsp **salt**
¼ tsp **black pepper**

Makes 4 servings
Calories: 319 per serving

Heat olive oil in a large griddle over medium-high heat. Add the garlic and fry for 1 minute, then stir in the tomatoes and cook for another 3 minutes.

Add the chickpeas, pasta, and basil. Season with salt and pepper. Cook for another 3 minutes.

Transfer the pasta mixture to a serving bowl. Sprinkle with vinegar, cheese and basil.

Enjoy!

18. Pork with Olives and Dijon

The olive-mustard tapenade adds an interesting flavor to this pork dish.

1 lb. (450 g) **pork tenderloin** (trimmed, cut)
½ tsp bottled **garlic** (minced)
¼ tsp **fennel** (ground)
½ cup **green olives** (chopped)
1 tbs **fresh parsley** (chopped)
1 tbs **Dijon mustard**
2 tsp **balsamic vinegar**
½ tsp **salt**
¼ tsp **black pepper**
Cooking spray

Makes 4 servings
Calories: 155 per serving

Heat olive oil in a nonstick skillet over medium-high heat.

Cut the pork into round ½-inch (1 cm) pieces. Combine the salt, pepper, and fennel, then evenly season the pork with it. Drizzle the pork with cooking spray.

Heat olive oil in a griddle over medium heat. Add the seasoned pork and roast for 5 minutes on each side, or until it gets a golden crust and is cooked through.

In a small bowl, combine balsamic vinegar, Dijon mustard, green olives, garlic, and parsley. Place the pork on a serving dish, top with olive mixture and serve.

Enjoy!

19. Cretan Briam

Briam is a specialty from Crete – a potato-based bake, flavored with olive oil and fresh parsley. Whether you serve it warm or chilled, it is delicious either way.

4 medium **red onions** (sliced)
2 lbs. (900 g) **potatoes** (peeled, sliced)
6 **plum tomatoes** (pureed)
½ cup **olive oil**
4 large **zucchinis** (sliced)
Salt and **pepper**
2 tbs **parsley** (chopped)

Makes 4 servings
Calories: 252 per serving

Preheat the oven to 390°F (200°C).

Place the cur zucchini, potatoes, and red onions in a large rimmed baking dish. Top with the pureed tomatoes, drizzle with olive oil, and season with salt, pepper and parsley. Mix to coat.

Add ½ cup of water to the baking dish and transfer to the oven. Bake for 90 minutes, stirring occasionally. If necessary, add a little more water to prevent the mixture from drying out and sticking to the bottom.

Remove from the oven and adjust seasonings if needed. Allow to cool for 10 minutes before serving.

Enjoy!

20. Fish in Tomato Sauce

Mediterranean fish stakes with a large variety of Mediterranean ingredients. Choose any fish you want.

5 oz. (150 g) **red onions** (thinly sliced)
2 **celery** sticks (thinly sliced)
1 **garlic** clove (thinly sliced)
1 **lemon** (thinly sliced)
1 tbs **dry white wine**
1 tbs **tomato purée**
2 tsp **olive oil**
4 **fish steaks** (5 oz. / 140 g each)
1 ¼ lbs. (570 g) **tomatoes** (chopped)
3 sprigs **rosemary**
3 tbs fresh **oregano** (chopped)
Salt and **pepper**

Makes 4 servings
Calories: 250 per serving

Heat the olive oil in an ovenproof skillet. Add the wine, onions, garlic, and celery. Sauté for about 5 minutes, or until softened.

Add the tomatoes, lemon, and tomato puree. Stir to combine. Bring the mixture to a boil, then reduce the heat and let simmer for about 3 minutes, or until tomatoes are tender.

Place the fish steaks in a single layer over the vegetable mixture and add the rosemary. Season with salt, pepper and oregano to taste.

Cover and let the mixture simmer for about 12 minutes, or until the sauce has thickened. Transfer to a serving dish, optionally garnish with some chopped rosemary and oregano and serve.

Enjoy!

21. Ratatouille

Ratatouille is a French stewed vegetable dish. It is done in less than an hour.

1 large **eggplant** (trimmed and diced)
2 medium **zucchini** (trimmed and diced)
1 medium **onion** (diced)
2 large fresh **tomatoes** (chopped)
2 cloves **garlic** (minced)
3 tbs **olive oil**
½ tsp dried **thyme**
¼ cup fresh **basil** (chopped)
¼ tsp dried **rosemary**
¼ tsp dried **marjoram**
¾ tsp **salt**
½ tsp ground **black pepper**

Makes 4 servings
Calories: 180 per serving

In a large nonstick sauce pan, heat 1 tbs olive oil over medium-high heat. Add the eggplant and stir cook for about 5 minutes, or until softened. Set aside.

Add the onion and another tbs of oil in the same heated pan. Sauté for about 5 minutes until softened and translucent. Stir in the zucchini and garlic and stir cook for 7 more minutes, or until softened.

Return the eggplant to the pan and stir in Herbes de Provence, tomatoes, salt and pepper to taste. Simmer for about 10 minutes. Mix in basil and the remaining tbs of oil.

Enjoy!

22. Curry Salmon with Basmati Rice

The Mediterranean cuisine is great when it comes to seafood. This is a healthy salmon recipe with rice, curry, mint, and cabbage.

2 tbs **olive oil**
Salt and **pepper** (ground)
1 lb. (450 g) **carrots** (grated)
2 tsp **curry powder**
½ cup **mint leaves**
1 cup brown **basmati rice**
¼ cup **lime juice**
4 **salmon fillets** (6 oz. / 170g each)
1 lb. (450 g) **Napa cabbage** (thinly sliced)

Makes 4 servings
Calories 374 per serving

Bring 2 cups of water to a boil in a large saucepan over medium heat. Add the rice, sprinkle with salt and pepper, cover and reduce heat to medium-low. Cook for about 30 minutes, or until all water is absorbed.

Meanwhile, in a large bowl, combine carrots, cabbage, lime juice and mint. Drizzle with oil and season with salt and pepper. Toss to coat.

Heat a broiler. Place the salmon steaks on a baking sheet lined with foil. Season the salmon with curry, salt and pepper. Broil for about 6 minutes, or until cooked through.

Transfer the cooked rice to a serving plate, then add the salmon and salad.

Enjoy!

Section 3: Salad Recipes

Vegetable Salads

1. Cucumber Salad with Tomato and Olives

This is a flavorful variation of a classic cucumber salad. It can easily be altered by substituting some of the ingredients. It is prepared in about 15 minutes.

Salad:
2 large **cucumbers** (diced)
½ red **onion** (thinly sliced)
3 large **tomatoes** (diced)
1 cup **Kalamata olives** (chopped)
2 tbs **rosemary** (chopped)
2 tsp **thyme leaves**
2 tsp **cilantro leaves**

Dressing:
1 tbs **balsamic vinegar**
3 tbs **red wine vinegar**
½ tsp **honey**
½ **lemon** (juiced)
1 ½ tsp **lemon** zest
1 ¼ tsp **salt** (or to taste)
¼ tsp ground **black pepper**
½ cup **olive oil**

Makes 6 servings
Calories: 235 per serving

In two separate bowls, combine the ingredients for the salad and dressing. Mix each to blend well.

Pour dressing over the salad. Toss to coat and serve immediately.

2. Mediterranean Vegetable Salad

This salad has a lot of flavor and combines many of the tastes and health benefits known from Mediterranean food.

¼ cup **green olives** (sliced)
2 tbs **olive oil**
2 oz. (50 g) **feta cheese** (crumbled)
½ cup **basil leaves**
1 tbs **vinegar**
1 pinch **salt** and **black pepper** (to taste)
4 cups **vegetables** (chopped):
Onions
Carrots
Tomatoes
Bell peppers
Zucchini
Cucumbers

Makes 4 servings
Calories: 135 per serving

In a large salad bowl, combine all of the ingredients. Toss well to blend.

For the vegetable mix, feel free to experiment with other combinations.

Enjoy!

3. Vegetable Salad in Italian Dressing

This salad contains a combination of fresh vegetables soaked in Italian seasoning and vinegar vinaigrette. It is best served 4 hours after preparing it.

2 tsp **Italian seasoning**
½ tsp **oregano** (dried)
½ clove **garlic** (minced)
½ tsp **basil** (dried)
½ tsp **rosemary** (dried)
½ tsp **marjoram** (dried)
½ cup **white vinegar**
½ cup **olive oil**
Fresh vegetables (of choice)
½ tsp **salt** and **pepper**

Makes 8 servings
Calories: 142 per serving

In a large salad bowl, combine all ingredients except the vegetables. Whisk to blend.

Add a mix of vegetables to the dressing. Toss and refrigerate for at least 4 hours.

Enjoy!

4. Honey Vegetable Salad

This is an appetizing salad made with honey and mustard dressing. It needs at least 6 hours of refrigeration for the flavors to develop well.

1 tbs arrowroot **flour**
½ cup **white wine vinegar**
¾ cup **honey**
1 tsp prepared **mustard**
8 oz. (225 g) **mixed vegetables** (of choice)
15 oz. (30 g) **red beans** (drained, rinsed)
¼ cup **celery** (chopped)
¼ cup **green bell pepper** (chopped)
¼ cup **onion** (chopped)

Makes 8 servings
Calories: 126 per serving

In a small pan, mix flour with vinegar, honey, and mustard. Bring to a boil over medium heat, then set aside to cool.

In a mixing bowl, combine the rest of the ingredients. Pour cooled dressing over vegetable mixture and toss to combine.

Chill for at least 6 hours before serving.

Enjoy!

5. Cucumber Salad with Feta Cheese

This salad is a variation of a classic Greek recipe with cucumbers carrying the exquisite flavors of herbs, wine vinegar and feta cheese.

1 ½ lb. (675 g) **cucumbers** (quartered, sliced)
3 tbs **olive oil**
2 tbs red **wine vinegar**
2 tbs **mint** (chopped)
1 tsp **oregano** (chopped)
½ cup **red onion** (thinly sliced)
2 tbs **dill** (chopped)
½ cup **feta** (crumbled)
Salt and ground **black pepper**

Makes 6 servings
Calories: 117 per serving

In a large bowl, combine cucumbers with vinegar, dill, mint, onion, and oregano. Toss to coat.

Add salt and pepper to taste.

Drizzle with olive oil and toss to coat again. Sprinkle feta cheese on top.

Serve and enjoy!

6. Garbanzo Bean Salad

The different textures and flavors of this salad go well together, while its colors appeal to the eyes. It is a delicious dish best served after at least 4 hours of refrigeration.

20 oz. (570 g) **garbanzo beans** (drained, rinsed)
¼ cup **parsley** (chopped)
1 large **red onion** (diced)
2 large **yellow bell peppers** (diced)
2 large **red bell peppers** (diced)
1 **jalapeno pepper** (diced)
Salt and ground **black pepper** (to taste)
¼ cup **olive oil**
1 **lemon** (juiced)
1 **lime** (juiced)

Makes 8 servings
Calories: 158 per serving

In a salad bowl, combine the first 6 ingredients. Toss to combine. Sprinkle salt and pepper to taste.

In a smaller bowl, whisk the rest of the ingredients until smooth. Pour over the salad and toss to blend. Chill for at least 4 hours before serving.

Enjoy!

7. Mediterranean Triple Salad

This Mediterranean salad combines three types of beans. It is a very refreshing salad even without refrigeration. The preparation time is just 15 minutes.

2 cloves **garlic** (minced)
2 tbs fresh **parsley** (minced) (to taste)
½ **onion** (minced)
15 oz. (425 g) **white kidney beans**
15 oz. (425 g) **garbanzo beans**
15 oz. (425 g) **red kidney beans**
1 **lemon** (juiced)
¼ cup **olive oil**
Salt and ground **black pepper** (to taste)

Makes 8 servings
Calories: 159 per serving

Combine all of the ingredients in a salad bowl. Gently toss to blend.

Let it rest for a few minutes before serving.

Enjoy!

8. Carrot Salad

Carrots are very healthy, but eating them raw is no way to really enjoy them. This salad is one of the best ways to it.

2 cloves **garlic**
2 lbs. (900 g) **carrots** (peeled, julienned)
2 tbs fresh **lemon juice**
1 tbs **white vinegar**
1/8 tsp **cayenne**
½ cup **olive oil**
¼ cup **chives** (minced)
¼ tsp **coriander seeds**
¼ tsp **cardamom seeds**
¼ tsp **fennel seeds**
¼ tsp **mustard seeds**
1 tsp **salt**
Ground **black pepper** (to taste)

Makes 8 servings
Calories: 264 per serving

Grind the seeds in a spice grinder. Crush garlic with salt and pepper in a mortar and pestle (or by other means available to you).

In a bowl, combine ground seeds, the garlic paste and the rest of the ingredients. Mix to combine. Chill for at least 1 hour.

Adjust seasonings to taste and serve with chives as garnish.

Enjoy!

9. Tomato Rosemary Salad

The different sizes of the tomatoes add to variety of this cold and appetizing salad. It is ready in about 25 minutes.

3 small **tomatoes** (quartered)
3 large **tomatoes** (quartered)
1/8 tsp **oregano** (dried)
2 tbs **white vinegar**
1 sprig **rosemary** (finely chopped)
¼ cup **olive oil**
Salt and ground **black pepper** (to taste)

Makes 8 servings
Calories: 155 per serving

In a salad bowl, mix olive oil with vinegar, oregano, and rosemary.

Add the tomatoes and toss to coat. Cover and chill for about 15 minutes.

Adjust seasoning to taste.

Serve and enjoy!

10. Quick Tomato Salad

This is the fastest way to prepare a simple yet, deliciously nourishing tomato salad. It is ready in 10 minutes.

1 large **tomato** (cut into wedges)
1 tbs **basil** (chopped)
1 tbs **olive oil**
1 ½ tsp **red wine vinegar** (to taste)
1 pinch **salt** and ground **black pepper** (to taste)

Makes 1 servings
Calories: 134 per serving

Simply combine everything in a salad bowl and toss to coat.

Enjoy!

Fruit Salads

1. Pearpom Salad with Greens

This salad combines the flavors of pears and pomegranates with watercress and lettuce. It is done in 15 minutes.

¼ cup **olive oil**
2 tbs **walnut oil**
½ tsp **Dijon mustard**
3 tbs **pomegranate juice**
3 tbs **white wine vinegar**
1 head **butter lettuce**
2 bunches **watercress** (trimmed)
2 **pears** (halved, cored, cut into wedges)
½ cup **ricotta cheese** (optional)
½ cup **pomegranate kernels**
Salt and **pepper** (to taste)

Makes 6 servings
Calories: 217 per serving

In a bowl, whisk oils with mustard, vinegar and pomegranate juice. Add salt and pepper to taste.

In a large salad bowl, combine lettuce and watercress. Add about 2 tbs of the dressing. Toss to coat.

Place greens on 6 serving plates. Arrange 4 pear wedges on each plate, drizzle another 2 tbs of the dressing, sprinkle optional cheese and top with pomegranate kernels.

Enjoy!

2. Peach Salad

Mangos and nectarines are good substitutes for the peaches, if you wish to give this salad another basis. It is ready in about 15 minutes.

1 lb. (450 g) ripe **peaches** (diced)
2 tsp **balsamic vinegar**
2 tsp **lemon juice**
3 tbs **olive oil**
1 large **tomato** (cubed)
1 small **red onion** (halved, sliced)
1/3 cup **cilantro** leaves
1 tsp **honey**
½ tsp **salt**
¼ tsp **black pepper**

Makes 4 servings
Calories: 175 per serving

In a salad bowl, whisk honey, vinegar and lemon juice until smooth. Add salt and pepper to taste. Gradually add oil, whisking until well blended.

Add the peach cubes and the rest of the ingredients. Toss to coat.

Enjoy!

3. Watermelon Salad

Watermelons are a great refreshment on hot days. This simple salad is even better! It can be prepared in about 40 minutes.

2 lbs. (900 g) **watermelon** (seeded, diced)
1 **lime zest** (finely grated)
2 tsp **lime juice**
1 tbs **cilantro leaves** (chopped)

Makes 2 servings
Calories: 135 per serving

In a salad bowl, combine all ingredients and toss to combine. Chill for 30 minutes before serving.

Enjoy!

4. Pear Salad with Bacon and Cheese

This pear salad is packed with greens, cheese, peppers and bacon, making it a rich meal by itself.

10 slices thick-cut **bacon** (diced)
¼ cup **balsamic vinegar**
6 tbs **olive oil**
4 cups **baby spinach** leaves
1 **Anjou pear** (peeled, cored, sliced)
¾ cup **Asiago cheese** (grated)
½ cup **red bell pepper** (diced)
2 tbs **shallot** (minced)
1/8 tsp ground **black pepper**
¼ tsp **sea salt**

Makes 4 servings
Calories: 426 per serving

In a pan, brown bacon over medium high heat for about 10 minutes, or until crisp. Drain on paper towel. Crumble and set aside.

In a small bowl, make the dressing by whisking oil with vinegar and adding salt and pepper.

In a large bowl, put spinach and drizzle with half of the dressing. Toss to coat.

Equally divide spinach into 4 plates. Layer the following in exact order on each plate: pear slices, bacon bits, cheese crumbles, minced shallots, diced bell peppers and drizzles of the remaining dressing.

Serve and enjoy!

5. Tropical Salad

This salad is a tropical treat that can be prepared in about 15 minutes.

2 **bananas** (sliced)
½ cup **pomegranate** seeds
3 tbs **coconut flesh** (shredded)
1 large **pineapple** (cored and chopped)
2 ripe **mangoes** (chopped)
½ cup **lychees** (chopped)
1 tsp **honey**

Makes 8 servings
Calories: 121 per serving

In a salad bowl, combine all ingredients except coconut. Toss to mix.

Heat a pan over medium flame and toast the shredded coconut for about 2 minutes, or until golden brown.

Garnish salad with toasted coconut before serving.

Enjoy!

6. Apple Chestnut Salad

This is a warm salad dish that combines chestnuts, apples, arugula and endive. It works very well as a side dish and is prepared in about 15 minutes after chilling the vegetables.

1 ½ cups steamed **chestnuts** (chopped)
1 ½ medium **apples**, (peeled, diced)
3 tbs **olive oil** (divided)
3 tbs **walnut oil**
¾ cup **shallots** (thinly sliced)
3 tbs **red wine vinegar**
6 cups **endive** (torn)
6 cups **arugula**

Makes 8 servings
Calories: 186 per serving

In a bowl, combine arugula with endive. Toss to mix. Cover with damp cloth and chill for at least 6 hours.

In a pan, heat 1 ½ tablespoons olive oil over medium-high heat. Sauté shallots and apples for about 5 minutes. Mix in chestnuts and sauté for 1 more minute. Add vinegar.

Remove from heat and mix in walnut oil and remaining olive oil. Sprinkle salt and pepper to taste. Pour the mixture over the chilled vegetables. Toss well and serve.

Enjoy!

7. Minty Fruit Salad

The secret of this salad lies in the mint. Its bright and refreshing flavor blends well with the sweetness of the fruits. It can be prepared in less than 10 minutes.

1 cup **apples** (cored, diced)
12 oz. (350 g) **blackberries**
¼ cup **mint** (finely chopped)
1 ½ cups **strawberries** (quartered)
¾ cup **pineapple** chunks

Makes 8 servings
Calories: 72 per serving

In a salad bowl, combine the fruits with the mint. Serve in individual bowls.

Enjoy!

8. Poppy Fruit Salad

Poppy seeds are added to this assembly of fresh fruits mainly to provide a contrasting texture. This salad works well if served with chicken dishes. For the best result, it needs 1 hour in the fridge after preparation.

Salad:
1 **banana** (peeled, sliced)
1 ½ cups **strawberries** (sliced, hulled)
2 cups **cantaloupe** (diced)
1 ½ cups **pineapple** (diced)
1 cup **seedless grapes** (halved)

Dressing:
2 tsp **white vinegar**
1 ¼ tsp **poppy seeds**
1/3 cup **Greek yogurt**
1/3 cup **sour cream** (optional)
2 tbs **honey**
3 tbs **ginger** (chopped)
Salt and **black pepper** (to taste)

Makes 4 servings
Calories: 256 per serving

In a bowl, combine all dressing ingredients. Whisk until smooth. Add salt and pepper to taste.

In a large salad bowl, combine all fruits. Pour dressing over it and toss to coat. Chill for about 1 hour before serving.

Enjoy!

9. Avocado-Mango Salad

Coarsely chopped fresh herbs and greens dominate the flavor of this salad. It contains passion fruit juice concentrate, which may be hard to come by but worth it. The outcome is a superb salad that is ready in 20 minutes.

2 tsp **red wine vinegar**
2 tsp **white wine vinegar**
1 tsp **Dijon mustard**
3 tbs **passion fruit concentrate**
3 tbs **shallot** (minced)
1 tsp **coriander seeds** (cracked)
3 tbs **olive oil**
8 cups **herb salad mix** (see below)
1 large **mango** (halved, sliced)
2 small **avocados** (halved, sliced)

Herb Salad Mix:
7 **oregano leaves** (chopped)
5 **thyme leaves** (chopped)
7 **basil leaves** (chopped)
1 cup **parsley** (chopped)
4 cups tender **lettuce** (chopped)

Makes 4 servings
Calories: 235 per serving

In a bowl, combine the two wine vinegars with mustard, passion fruit concentrate, shallot and coriander seeds. Whisk to blend while adding the olive oil. Add salt and pepper to taste.

In a large bowl, combine all ingredients for the herb salad mix. Pour in ¼ cup dressing and toss well.

Equally portion salad on 4 serving bowls. Add avocado and mango slices and drizzle remaining dressing.

Enjoy!

10. Melon Salad with Prosciutto

This is a melon salad with added protein from prosciutto ham, nutrients from greens and a kick from chili peppers.

1 **cantaloupe** (peeled, diced)
1 **honeydew melon** (peeled, diced)
1 **Sharlyn melon** (peeled, diced)
4 black **figs** (quartered)
1 bunch **basil leaves**
1 tbs **chili flakes** (for garnish)
4 oz. (115 g) **rocket greens**
8 oz. (225 g) **prosciutto di Parma** (julienned)
4 oz. (115 g) **ricotta salata** (shaved, for garnish)
1 tbs **olive oil**

Makes 4 servings
Calories: 145 per serving

On each of the 4 serving plates, place melon dices in the middle and layer prosciutto on top, followed by 8 micro basil leaves, 4 fig quarters and a some rocket leaves.

Shower with olive oil, sprinkle with ricotta cheese and top with chili flakes.

Enjoy!

Pasta Salads

1. Mediterranean Macaroni Salad

A quick and simple pasta salad lusciously flavored with olives, peppers and feta cheese. It is cooked and prepared in about 25 minutes.

1 cup **macaroni**
1 tbs **garlic** (minced)
1 tbs **olive oil**
¼ cup **black olives** (sliced)
2 oz. (50 g) **red bell peppers** (diced)
¼ cup **feta cheese** (crumbled)
1 tsp **lemon juice**
Salt and **pepper** to taste

Makes 2 servings
Calories: 325 per serving

In a pot of boiling salted water, cook pasta according to packaging instructions. Drain in a colander and rinse with cool water. Set aside in a bowl.

In a bowl, mix olive oil and garlic. Set aside.

Add red peppers, olives, and feta cheese to the pasta. Mix in lemon juice and the oil-garlic mixture. Season with salt and pepper to taste. Serve immediately.

Enjoy!

2. Rotini Salad with Spinach and Dill

This pasta salad can be served hot or cold and is ready in 30 minutes.

1 lb. (450 g) **rotini pasta**
3 tbs **olive oil**
3 cloves **garlic** (minced)
1 tbs **dill weed** (dried)
7 oz. (200 g) **feta cheese** (crumbled)
10 oz. (280 g) frozen **spinach** (chopped)
salt and **pepper** to taste

Makes 6 servings
Calories: 384 per serving

In a pot of boiling salted water, cook rotini pasta according to packaging instructions. Drain in a colander, rinse and set aside in a bowl.

While pasta is cooking, boil water in a saucepan. Add spinach and sauté for about 5 minutes, or until just wilted. Drain in a colander and set aside.

In a large pot, heat oil over medium heat and cook garlic until browned. Mix in spinach and pasta. Remove from heat and allow to cool for about 10 minutes.

Mix in dill and feta cheese. Serve immediately.

Enjoy!

3. Farfalle Pasta with Vegetables

A Greek pasta with roasted vegetables, feta cheese and arugula leaves. It can be prepared in about 40 minutes.

12 oz. (340 g) **farfalle pasta**
3 small **yellow squash** (sliced)
1 red **bell pepper** (chopped)
1 medium **eggplant** (cubed)
1 yellow **bell pepper** (chopped)
6 tbs **olive oil** (divided)
¼ tsp **salt** and ground **black pepper**
½ cup torn **arugula leaves**
2 tbs **balsamic vinegar**
2 tbs **garlic** (minced)
½ cup **fresh basil** (chopped)
4 oz. (110 g) **feta cheese** (crumbled)

Makes 6 servings
Calories: 318 per serving

Preheat oven to 450 °F (230 °C). Lightly grease a tin foil-lined cookie sheet.

In a bowl, combine the bell peppers, squash, and eggplant. Drizzle with 2 tbs olive oil and season with salt and pepper to taste. Place the mixture in one layer on the prepared cookie sheet and bake in the oven for about 25 minutes, or until just browned.

Meanwhile, cook pasta according to packaging instructions. Drain in a colander and set aside to cool.

Combine the arugula, basil, baked vegetables, cooked pasta, remaining olive oil, garlic, vinegar, and feta cheese. Mix well and serve immediately.

Enjoy!

4. Rotini Pasta with Olives and Fungi

Full of colors and rich in flavors, this pasta is ready in about 20 minutes.

8 oz. (225 g) **rotini pasta**
3 cups **mushrooms** (sliced)
16 **cherry tomatoes** (halved)
¾ cup **feta cheese** (crumbled)
4 oz. (110 g) **black olives** (chopped)
½ cup **green onions** (chopped)
½ cup **olive oil**
½ cup red **wine vinegar**
1 ½ tsp **oregano** (dried)
1 ½ tsp **garlic** powder
1 ½ tsp **basil leaves** (dried)

Makes 8 servings
Calories: 147 per serving

Cook pasta according to packaging instructions. Drain in a colander and set aside in a bowl.

Add the rest of the ingredients to the pasta bowl. Mix well and serve immediately.

Alternatively, allow the mix to cool, then cover and refrigerate for 3 hours to serve it chilled.

Enjoy!

5. Rotini Pasta with Beans and Cucumber

This Greek pasta salad combines garbanzo beans and cucumber with Mediterranean flavors. It is prepared in about 45 minutes.

12 oz. (340 g) **rotini pasta**
4 oz. (110 g) **black olives** (drained)
¼ red **onion** (finely diced)
1 lb. (450 g) **garbanzo beans**
10 oz. (280 g) **grape tomatoes** (halved)
1 **cucumber** (peeled, diced)
¼ cup **olive oil**
½ cup **feta cheese** (crumbled)
2 cloves **garlic** (diced)
1 tbs fresh **lemon juice**
1 tbs **balsamic vinegar**
1 tbs **basil** (chopped)
salt and ground **black pepper** (to taste)

Makes 4 servings
Calories: 287 per serving

Cook pasta according to packaging instructions. Drain in a colander and set aside in a bowl.

In a large salad bowl, combine the rest of the ingredients, except feta cheese. Add the pasta and mix well. Refrigerate for at least 30 minutes. Served chilled with cheese on top.

Enjoy!

6. Orzo Pasta Salad in Bell Peppers

For this dish, red bell peppers are stuffed with orzo pasta salad. It can be prepared in about 1 hour.

½ lb. (225 g) **orzo pasta**
1 grilled **chicken breast** half (diced)
1 tsp **Dijon mustard**
¼ cup **olive oil**
1/3 cup **red wine vinegar**
¾ tsp **oregano** (dried)
¾ tsp **basil** (dried)
¾ tsp **garlic powder**
¾ tsp **onion powder**
2 oz. (55 g) **feta cheese** (crumbled)
½ cup **grape tomatoes** (halved)
¼ cup **black olives** (halved)
2 red **bell peppers** (halved, seeded)
½ tsp **salt**
¼ tsp ground **black pepper**

Makes 4 servings
Calories: 326 per serving

Cook pasta according to packaging instructions. Drain in a colander and set aside in a bowl.

In a bowl, combine olive oil, onion powder, oregano, garlic powder, basil, Dijon mustard, and red wine vinegar. Mix and season with salt and pepper.

In a separate bowl, mix the pasta with the rest of the ingredients except bell pepper halves. Add the dressing and toss to coat.

Stuff bell peppers with the pasta salad and serve.

Enjoy!

7. Quinoa Salad in Marinade

This is a flavorful and protein-packed side dish. It can be prepared in about 3.5 hours.

Dish:
1 lb. (450 g) **cherry tomatoes** (halved)
1 cup **quinoa**
6 oz. (170 g) **black olives** (sliced)
1/3 cup sun-dried **tomato** (chopped)
2 red **onions** (chopped)
¾ cup **pine nuts** (toasted)

Marinade:
2 tbs **olive oil**
2 tbs **balsamic vinegar**
3 tbs **lemon juice**
4 tbs **orange juice**
1 tsp **honey**
½ cup **basil leaf** (chopped)
½ tsp **garlic powder**
Salt and ground **black pepper**

Makes 7 servings
Calories: 354 per serving

In a colander, wash quinoa under running water. Add to a pot of boiling water and let simmer for about 15 minutes, or until translucent. Remove from heat, drain in the colander and allow to cool in a bowl.

In a separate bowl, combine all ingredients for the marinade. Add to the cooled quinoa and mix well.

Add all the herbs and vegetables. Scatter pine nuts on top, cover and refrigerate for 3 hours.

8. Orzo Pasta with Spinach

A Mediterranean salad with baby spinach leaves. It is ready in about 20 minutes.

8 oz. (225 g) **orzo pasta**
2 cups **cherry tomatoes** (halved)
2 cups **baby spinach** leaves
¼ cup **pine nuts** (toasted)
½ cup **Kalamata olive** (pitted and halved)
1 cup **basil leaf** (chopped)
1 tsp **garlic** (minced)
4 oz. (110 g) **feta cheese** (diced)
2 tbs **balsamic vinegar**
1 tbs **olive oil**
Salt and ground **black pepper**

Makes 8 servings
Calories: 195 per serving

Cook pasta according to packaging instructions. Drain in a colander and set aside in a bowl.

While the pasta is cooking, combine cherry tomatoes with the next six ingredients down to feta cheese. Add the cooled pasta.

In a small bowl, mix vinegar and olive oil, then season with salt and pepper to taste. Pour over the salad and toss to coat.

Enjoy!

9. Pasta Salad with Italian Dressing

This pasta is packed with vegetables and is meant to be served on gatherings with many mouths to feed. It is prepared in 40 minutes and needs to be refrigerated overnight.

12 oz. (340 g) **spiral pasta**
1 lb. (450 g) **rotini pasta**
14 oz. (400 g) **mushrooms** (sliced)
15 oz. (425 g) **cannellini beans**
13 oz. (360 g) **black olives**
13 oz. (360 g) **artichokes** (quartered)
3 **roma tomatoes** (seeded, cubed)
4 **radishes** (halved, sliced)
1 small **red onion** (cut into strips)
1 yellow **bell pepper** (chopped)
2 **garlic** cloves
½ cup **parmesan cheese** (shredded)
12 oz. (340 g) **Italian salad dressing**
Salt and black **pepper** (to taste)

Makes 28 servings
Calories: 165 per serving

Cook pasta according to packaging instructions. Drain in a colander.

In a large salad bowl, combine pasta with the next ingredients down to parmesan cheese.

Add ¾ of the Italian salad dressing and toss to coat. Season with salt and pepper. Cover and refrigerate overnight.

Before serving, add the remaining salad dressing and toss to coat.

10. Lemony Pasta with Artichoke Hearts

This pasta salad is prepared in about 2 hours and 20 minutes.

4 oz. (110 g) **orzo pasta**
2 tbs **butter** or **coconut butter**
2 tsp **Italian seasoning**
1 cup **onion** (chopped)
2 cups green **bell peppers** (chopped)
14 oz. (400 g) **artichoke hearts** (quartered)
½ cup **cucumber** (chopped)
¼ cup **black olives** (halved)
¼ cup **parsley** (chopped)
1 ½ cups **tomatoes** (chopped)
2 tbs **lemon juice**
½ tsp **salt**

Makes 6 servings
Calories: 183 per serving

Cook pasta according to packaging instructions. Drain in a colander and set aside in a bowl to cool.

While pasta is cooking, heat the butter of your choice in a pan. Add onion, bell peppers, and Italian seasoning and cook for about 6 minutes, or until tender.

In a salad bowl, mix pasta with the pepper mixture and all remaining ingredients. Toss to coat, cover and refrigerate for at least 2 hours.

Serve and enjoy!

Meat & Seafood Salads

1. Tarragon Pasta Salad with Capers

This is a classic chicken salad boasting with Mediterranean flavors. It can be prepared in 20 minutes.

½ cup **orzo pasta**
6 oz. (170 g) **artichoke hearts** (chopped)
½ tbs **Dijon mustard**
6 tbs **olive oil**
1 tbs **tarragon**
4 tbs **tarragon vinegar**
½ tbs **lemon juice**
3 cups **cooked chicken** (diced)
1 cup **cherry tomatoes** (halved)
1/3 cup **currant** (dried)
1 ½ tbs **capers**

Makes 4 servings
Calories: 386 per serving

Cook pasta according to packaging instructions. Drain in a colander and set aside to cool.

In a bowl, combine Dijon mustard, olive oil, lemon juice, tarragon, and vinegar. Season with salt and pepper to taste.

Add chicken dices, pasta, artichoke hearts, tomatoes, currant, and capers to the bowl. Mix to blend. If needed, season with more salt and pepper to taste.

Enjoy!

2. Sirloin Salad with Vinaigrette

This is a juicy salad with meat and feta cheese. It is done in about 35 minutes.

Salad:
1 lb. (450 g) **top sirloin steak**
½ small **red onion** (sliced)
½ cup **feta cheese** (crumbled)
1 cup **cherries** (halved)
4 cups **romaine leaves** (torn)
¼ tsp **salt**
1/8 tsp **black pepper**

Lemon vinaigrette:
1 tbs **oregano** (crushed)
2 **garlic** cloves (minced)
¼ cup **olive oil**
½ tsp **lemon peel** (shredded)
3 tbs **lemon juice**
Salt and **black pepper**

Makes 4 servings
Calories: 345 per serving

Preheat a broiler.

Rub trimmed steak with salt and pepper. Place on a rack and broil for about 20 minutes, turning once.

Meanwhile, prepare vinaigrette by mixing all ingredients in a bowl. Season with salt and black pepper to taste.

Once done, thinly slice the broiled steak into thin slices.

Equally divide romaine leaves on 4 serving plates. Top with steak slices, followed by red onion, tomatoes, and feta cheese. Drizzle with vinaigrette.

Enjoy!

3. Grilled Steak Salad

This salad features grilled flank steaks mixed with salad greens and balsamic vinaigrette. It is done in about 30 minutes.

12 oz. (340 g) any **flank steaks** (trimmed)
1/3 cup **balsamic vinaigrette**
8 oz. (225 g) mixed **salad greens**
1 large **tomato** (cut in chunks)
2 ½ oz. (70 g) **green olives** (sliced)

Balsamic Vinaigrette:
¾ cup **olive oil**
1 small clove **garlic** (minced)
3 tbs **balsamic vinegar**
2 tsp **Dijon mustard**
1 tsp. kosher **salt** (more to taste)
About 5 grinds **black pepper** (more to taste)

Spice Rub:
¼ tsp ground **cinnamon**
1 tsp **garlic** powder
1 tsp ground **oregano**
1 tsp **salt** and ¼ tsp **pepper**

Makes 4 servings
Calories: 179 per serving

Preheat a grill.

In a bowl, combine the ingredients for the spice rub. Mix to blend, then set aside.
In another bowl, combine the ingredients for the vinaigrette. Add ½ cup water and 1 tsp spice rub. Mix to blend, then set aside.

Add remaining spice rub to both sides of the steak. Grill for about 5 minutes per side for rare doneness.
Transfer to a cutting board and slice thinly, then cover and let stand for another 5 minutes.

In a salad bowl, add mixed salad greens of your choice, steak slices and all remaining ingredients. Drizzle vinaigrette and toss to coat.

4. Tuna Salad with Green Beans

This Mediterranean salad uses Dijon mustard, whisked in olive oil and vinegar to blend tuna with greens. It is ready in 35 minutes.

10 oz. (280 g) **tuna**
1 ½ lbs. (680 g) small **yellow potatoes**
30 **red** and **yellow cherry tomatoes** (halved)
½ lb. (225 g) **green beans** (trimmed)
2 tbs **Dijon mustard**
¼ cup **olive oil**
2 tbs **red wine vinegar**
2 tbs **capers** (drained)
4 cups **baby lettuce**

Makes 6 servings
Calories: 221 per serving

In a pot of boiling water, cook potatoes for about 15 minutes, or until fork tender. Drain in a colander, rinse and cool. Cut in halves.

In a microwave oven, cook green beans for about 5 minutes, or until just softened. Rinse with running water.

In a small bowl, mix olive oil, mustard and vinegar. Whisk until smooth. Mix in capers and set aside.

In a large bowl, combine tuna with potatoes, tomatoes, lettuce, and green beans. Drizzle the dressing over the salad. Toss to coat.

Enjoy!

5. Chicken Salad with Yoghurt

This is a chicken salad with tarragon and celery. It can be prepared in 70 minutes.
Note: For a less healthy but tasty alternative, you can try adding 1 tsp mayonnaise to the yoghurt.

3 cups cooked **chicken** (diced)
½ cup **Greek yogurt**
¼ cup **green onions** (chopped)
1 ½ tsp **tarragon** (dried)
1 ½ cups **celery** (chopped)
2 tbs **slivered almonds** (toasted)
Salt and **pepper** (to taste)

Makes 6 servings
Calories: 147 per serving

In a bowl, combine all ingredients, except toasted almonds. Toss to coat, then refrigerate for 1 hour.

Adjust seasoning and serve with almonds on top.

Enjoy!

6. Diverse Shrimp Salad

A light but well-packed salad with greens, beans, avocado, cucumber, olives, feta cheese and topped with sautéed shrimp. It is done in 20 minutes.

1 lb (450 g) **shrimps** (shelled, tails removed)
¼ tsp hot **pepper flakes**
1 tbs **olive oil**
1 **garlic** clove (crushed)

¼ cup **green olives** (sliced)
2 **tomatoes** (cut in wedges)
14 oz. (400 g) **garbanzo beans**
½ **cucumber** (peeled, sliced)
1 **avocado** (diced)
6 cups **romaine lettuce** (torn)
4 green **onions**
¼ cup **feta cheese** (crumbled)
Greek salad dressing

Makes 4 servings
Calories: 366 per serving

In a pan, heat olive oil over medium heat. Sauté garlic and pepper flakes for about 2 minutes. Add shrimps and sauté for another 3 minutes, or until opaque. Set aside.

In a large salad bowl, combine the remaining ingredients. Mix to coat. Serve in small bowls with sautéed shrimps on top.

Enjoy!

7. Crab Salad with Goat Cheese

This is a crab salad with Mediterranean flavors. It is ready in 25 minutes.

6 oz. (170 g) **artichoke hearts** (quartered)
1 lb (450 g) backfin **crab meat**
¼ cup **green onions** (chopped)
4 tbs **lemon juice** (freshly squeezed)
1 ½ tsp **Dijon mustard**
¼ tsp **oregano**
2/3 cup **olive oil**
½ cup **black olives** (sliced)
7 oz. (200 g) **red peppers** (roasted)
6 cups mixed **greens**
½ cup **goat cheese** (crumbled, divided)
½ tsp **salt and pepper** (to taste)

Makes 6 servings
Calories: 398 per serving

In a bowl, combine green onions with mustard, oregano and lemon juice. Whisk with oil until blended. Add salt and pepper to taste. Reserve 1/3 cup of the dressing for later use.

Mix in crab meat, olives, roasted peppers and artichoke hearts. Set aside.

In a large salad bowl, combine greens with half of the goat cheese. Drizzle reserved dressing and toss to coat.

Place greens on top the crab meat mixture. Sprinkle with the remaining cheese.

Enjoy!

8. Calamari Salad

This calamari salad makes a sufficient meal or a substantial side dish. It is ready in 25 minutes and best served with Greek yogurt and pita bread.

1 lb (450 g) **calamari** (sliced)
½ cup **Kalamata olives** (pitted, sliced)
2 tbs **capers** (chopped)
2 cups **tomatoes** (chopped)
1 tbs **lemon juice**
2 tbs **parsley** (chopped)
2 **garlic** cloves (minced)
1 tbs **lemon rind** (finely grated)
½ cup **arrowroot flour**
¼ tsp **salt** and **black pepper**
½ cup **almonds** (ground)
1 ¼ cups **breadcrumbs**
2 **eggs** (beaten)
8 cups **canola oil**
Salad greens

Makes 6 servings
Calories: 425 per serving

In a bowl, combine parsley, olives, capers, salt & pepper, garlic, tomatoes, and lemon juice. Mix well to blend. Set aside.

Prepare 3 shallow bowls. Whisk flour and lemon rind in the first bowl. Beat eggs in the second bowl. Mix almonds and breadcrumbs in the third bowl.

Heat olive oil in a pan over medium-high heat. Pass calamari in batches from the first to the last bowl and fry for 1-2 minutes, or until golden brown. Drain on a paper towel.

Combine salad greens with the mixture from the beginning. Top with calamari.

Enjoy!

9. Green Salad with Sardines

This is a quick but nutritious green salad with intense sardine flavor. It can be prepared in about 15 minutes.

4 oz (120 g) can **sardines in tomato sauce**
1 cup **salad greens**
½ cup **green olives** (chopped)
1 tbs **caper** (drained)
1 tbs **olive oil**
1 tbs **red wine vinegar**

Makes 4 servings
Calories: 146 per serving

Place salad greens on 4 plates, then top with capers and olives.

Remove sardines from the can, reserving the tomato sauce. Shred sardines into pieces, then add to the salad.

In a bowl, mix the reserved tomato sauce with vinegar and olive oil, then pour over the salad.

Enjoy!

10. Orzo Salad with Salmon

12 oz. (340 g) **salmon fillets**
½ cup **orzo** (uncooked)
¼ tsp **oregano** (dried)
2 cups **spinach** (torn)
4 **Kalamata olives** (chopped)
3 tbs **lemon juice**
½ cup **red bell pepper** (chopped)
¼ cup **green onions** (chopped)
2 tbs **feta cheese** (crumbled)
¼ tsp **salt**
1/8 tsp **black pepper**

Makes 4 servings
Calories: 222 per serving

Preheat broiler. Lightly grease a broiler pan.

Cook pasta according to packaging instructions. Drain in a colander and set aside in a bowl to cool.

While pasta is cooking, season salmon with oregano, salt and pepper. Place on prepared pan and broil for about 10 minutes, or until flaky. Shred into coarse bits.

In a salad bowl, combine pasta, salmon, spinach, and remaining ingredients. Toss well before serving.

Enjoy!

11. Prawn Pasta Salad

A delicious salad with prawns, pasta and apple bits that is prepared and chilled in 2 hours and 30 minutes.

8 oz. (225 g) **red apples** (peeled, diced)
8 oz. (225 g) cooked **prawns** (shelled)
6 oz. (175 g) **pasta shells**
1 tsp **mint** (chopped)
1 tsp **white wine vinegar**
½ cup **apple juice**
Lettuce leaf (finely sliced)
Paprika (to garnish)
Salt and **pepper** (to taste)

Makes 6 servings
Calories: 164 per serving

Cook pasta according to packaging instructions. Drain in a colander and set aside in a bowl to cool.

In a bowl, mix vinegar with apple juice and mint. Add salt and pepper to taste. Set aside.

In a salad bowl, combine prawns and apples, then coat with previous mixture. Cover and refrigerate for 2 hours.

Divide lettuce on serving plates and top with the salad. Garnish with paprika.

Enjoy!

12. Pasta Salad with Scallops and Oranges

This is a refreshing salad filled with citrus flavors and the distinct taste of scallops. It is ready in about 25 minutes.

¾ lb (340 g) **pasta**
2 **oranges** (peeled, chopped)
1 lb (450 g) **sea scallops**
5 tbs **olive oil**
1 tbs **lemon juice**
½ cup **Kalamata olives** (pitted)
½ small **red onion** (chopped finely)
6 tbs **mint** (chopped)
Salt and **black pepper** (to taste)

Makes 4 servings
Calories: 460 per serving

Cook pasta according to packaging instructions. Drain in a colander and set aside in a bowl to cool.

Season scallops with salt and pepper to taste.

In a pan, heat olive oil over medium flame. Cook scallops in batches for about 2 minutes per side or until browned.

In a salad bowl, combine chopped orange pieces and the rest of the ingredients. Season with salt and pepper to taste. Add the pasta and scallops, then mix.

Enjoy!

13. Lemony Seafood Salad

In this salad, calamari, shrimp and scungilli are marinated with lemon juice and flavored with Mediterranean ingredients. It is prepared in 1 hour and 10 minutes.

1 ½ lbs. (680 g) **calamari rings**
1 lb. (450 g) **shrimp** (cooked, shelled)
30 oz. (855 g) **scungilli** (sliced conch)
6 oz. (170 g) **green olives** (halved)
15 sprigs **parsley** (chopped)
1 clove **garlic** (minced)
2 handfuls **capers** (salted)
5 pieces **celery stalks** (sliced)
2 **lemons** (juiced)
2 tbs **olive oil**
salt and **pepper** to taste

Makes 8 servings
Calories: 376 per serving

Cook calamari in boiling water for about 1 minute. Drain in a colander and rinse to cool.

In a large salad bowl, combine cooked calamari, shrimps, scungilli, olives, and parsley. Drizzle with lemon juice and olive oil, then toss to coat.

Add salt and pepper to taste, then refrigerate for 1 hour.

Serve on plates and garnish with lemon wedges.

Enjoy!

14. Cod fillet Salad with

This cod salad is soaked in a delicious Mediterranean flavored sauce. It is prepared in about 45 minutes.

1 tbs **capers** (drained)
1 tbs **basil leaves** (julienned)
1 plum **tomato** (chopped)
1 **shallot** (minced)
¼ tsp **orange zest** (grated)
1 tsp **lemon juice**
2 tbs **olive oil** (divided)
1/3 cup **Kalamata olives** (diced)
2 x 6 oz. (170 g) pieces **cod fillet**
1 cup **salad greens**
Basil sprigs (garnish)
Salt and **black pepper**

Makes 2 servings
Calories: 288 per serving

In a bowl, combine tomato, capers, shallot, basil, orange zest, lemon juice, olives, and 1 tbs olive oil. Mix well. Add salt and ground black pepper to taste. Set aside.

Rub cod fillets with salt. In a pan, heat the remaining 1 tbs olive oil over medium-high flame. Fry cod fillets for about 4 minutes on each side, or until golden brown.

Serve fillets on salad greens and pour mixture from the beginning. Garnish with basil sprigs.

Enjoy!

15. Lemony Anchovy Salad

This salad combines the taste of anchovies, red wine vinegar and lemons. It can be prepared in about 25 minutes.

8 oz. (225 g) **white anchovies**
3 tbs **red wine vinegar**
½ cup **olive oil**
5 oz. (150 g) **baby arugula**
½ small **red onion** (sliced, divided)
1 large **fennel bulb**, (sliced, divided)
1 **lemon** (minced)
Salt and **black pepper**

Makes 8 servings
Calories: 178 per serving

In a bowl, combine onion, fennel, arugula, and lemon.

In a small bowl, combine vinegar and olive oil, then season with salt and pepper to taste. Add mixture to the first bowl.

Divide mixture to serving plates and top with remaining fennel, onion, and anchovies.

Enjoy!

Salad Dressings

1. Greek Dressing

This is a basic recipe for Greek salad dressing. It works well for green salads and pasta and takes about 5 minutes to prepare.

2 tsp **onion powder**
1 tsp **mustard** (ground)
1 tsp **rosemary**
1 cup **olive oil**
3 tsp **garlic** powder
3 tsp dried **basil**
1 1/3 cups **red wine vinegar**
3 tsp dried **oregano**
2 tsp **salt** and **black pepper**

Makes 20 servings
Calories: 99 per serving

Combine all ingredients inside a lidded container. Shake briskly until well-mixed.

Seal and store at room temperature.

Enjoy!

2. Italian Dressing

This Italian dressing works well for green salads and pasta. It is done in 5 minutes.

¼ cup **cider vinegar**
¾ cup **vegetable oil**
1 tsp **parmesan cheese** (grated)
2 tsp **honey**
1 tsp **garlic** (minced)
2 tbs **water**
1 ½ tsp **salt**
¼ tsp **pepper**

Makes 4 servings
Calories: 103 per serving

Combine all ingredients inside a lidded container. Shake briskly until well-mixed.

Seal and store at room temperature.

Enjoy!

3. Italian Yoghurt Dressing

This Italian dressing is not only good for salad and pasta, it also works well with meat. It can be prepared in 5 minutes.

3 tsp **Italian seasoning**
1 tsp **Dijon mustard**
2 tsp **dry white wine**
2 tsp **red** or **white wine vinegar**
2 garlic **cloves**
1 tsp **honey**
1 cup **plain yoghurt**
1 tsp **parmesan cheese** (grated)
1 tsp **olive oil**
½ tsp **black pepper**

Makes 16 servings
Calories: 27 per serving

Combine all ingredients but the yoghurt. Mix until blended.

Add yoghurt and mix again until blended.

Enjoy!

4. Sweet Dressing

This is a simple dressing that is lightly sweetened to blend well with greens. It takes about 5 minutes to prepare.

½ cup **white wine vinegar**
2 small **garlic** cloves (minced)
1 cup **olive oil**
2 ½ tbs **honey**
½ tsp **salt** and **black pepper**

Makes 10 servings
Calories: 87 per serving

In a lidded container, mix all ingredients until well blended.

Enjoy!

5. Pistachio Dressing

This salad dressing contains the nutty taste of pistachios. It is about 5 minutes and works well with meat salads.

3 tbs **pistachios**
1½ tbs **olive oil**
1 handful flat-leaf **parsley leaves** (torn)
2 **dill** sprigs (torn)
1 pinch **Salt**

Makes 2 servings
Calories: 85 per serving

In a pan, toast pistachios over low medium heat for about 3 minutes, or until golden and crunchy.

Chop pistachios roughly. In a bowl, mix olive oil, parsley, dill, and pistachios. Season with a pinch of salt.

Enjoy!

Made in the USA
Lexington, KY
21 March 2015